MIKE,

SINCE YOUR GOAL THIS
YEAR IS TO GET A HOUSE. I
THOUGHT THIS BOOK WOULD
HELP YOU REACH YOUR GOAL.
WHAT GREAT MOTIVATING TOOL ♧ ! HUH?!
I HOPE ALL YOUR DREAMS & WISHES
COME TRUE! THINK BIG & DREAM
BIG & YOU WILL NEVER GO
WRONG! THIS IS YOUR SUMMER!!
REMEMBER THAT! KEEP STRONG!
"BANDIT"

-M-   5-24-05
Liz

HOUSTON HOME BOOK

A COMPREHENSIVE HANDS-ON DESIGN SOURCEBOOK FOR BUILDING, REMODELING, DECORATING, FURNISHING AND LANDSCAPING A LUXURY HOME IN HOUSTON AND SURROUNDING AREAS

Photo by **Rex Spencer**
Photo courtesy of **The Bryan Design Associates**

PUBLISHED BY

THE
ASHLEY
GROUP

Chicago   New York   Houston

Southeast Florida   Atlanta   Detroit

Arizona   Dallas/Fort Worth   San Diego

Philadelphia   San Francisco Bay Area   Colorado

Boston   Seattle   Kansas City   Orange County

Central Ohio   Connecticut/Westchester County

HOUSTON HOME BOOK

Published By
The Ashley Group
10900 Northwest Freeway, Suite 122
Houston, TX 77092
713-263-0471 Fax: 713-263-1927

Reed Business Information™
Reed Business Information
A Division of Reed Elsevier Inc

ISBN 1-58862-104-9

HOUSTON HOME BOOK
Publisher *Joe Pisano*
Editor-in-Chief *Dana Felmly*
Managing Editor *Laurence P. Maloney*
Senior Editor *James Scalzitti*
Assistant Editor *Erin N. Deener*
Listings Manager *Amanda Westbrooks*
Office Manager *Serena G. Perrilloux*
Account Executives *Shannon Perry, Vinny Celano*
Group Production Director *Paula Gordon*
Production Director *Paul Ojeda*
Production Manager *Kristen Axelson*
Creative Director *Bill Weaver*
Senior Graphic Designer *Maria T. Perez*
Graphic Designers *W. Keel, David Malec, Jennifer Morris,
Amie L. Smith, Andrew Stamm, Kate Uhler*
Ad Service Coordinator *Tom Kusmierz*
Project Coordinator *Tracy A. Potocki*
Prepress *Reed Prepress*
Printed in China by *Everbest Printing Company*

THE ASHLEY GROUP
**Executive Vice President,
General Manager of The Ashley Group** *Greg Samios*
Vice President of Sales *Ed Barnes*
Regional Director *Joseph Lattimer*
Group Controller *Patricia Lavigne*
Group Administration *Nicole Port, Kimberly Spizzirri*

REED BUSINESS INFORMATION
Chief Executive Officer *James Casella*
Chief Financial Officer *John Poulin*
Vice President, Finance *David Lench*

Front Cover *Photo courtesy of Designer Showcase*
Back Cover *Photo courtesy of Hann Builders. Photo by John Blackmer*

Editors' Note

Casual living, open floorplans, making one's design opinions known — all of these trends are oft-cited by today's housing professionals as the desires of their clients. But they are far from being the only ones. Creating one's home environment exactly as one wants it is more important than it has ever been. Our houses are our first vestige of shelter, our last dependable asset, and an investment which we can decorate and enjoy much better than a money market or stock portfolio!

In the two years since we, Dana Felmly and James Scalzitti, have stepped into our respective roles with The Ashley Group, we have developed the editorial content for Home Books in 18 U.S. markets. In that time, we've discovered how the desire for a better lifestyle affects design. For example, outdoor rooms — formal rooms with little or no wall structure — are popular in the West because of homeowners' desire to enjoy long, warm evenings outdoors. Mud rooms are specifically requested in the North and Midwest so that family and friends can remove their muddy boots and shoes in a warm environment away from the more formal rooms.

Literally anything that doesn't need an act of God (and even some things that do!) can be created for a home environment. It is up to you to know or sense what would make that environment perfect, and then express your desires to the professionals who can make them happen. They are looking to you for the inspiration to develop their next great project!

We've done our best to showcase some outstanding professionals. We can help you find them and give you advice on how to talk and work with them (see articles in the beginning of each tab section). Great ideas can be conceived simply by viewing the pictures in the articles, ads, and our new Award Show section, which highlights the winners of the local Design Excellence contest.

Somewhere inside you is the vision of your ideal home. If you don't yet know what it is, you are likely to find it here. And if you do know what it is, then you'll find a way in this book to make it better! So start flipping these pages — and good luck! If you have any questions, don't hesitate to e-mail us. We'd love to hear from you.

Dana Felmly
Editor-in-Chief
dfelmly@reedbusiness.com

James Scalzitti
Senior Editor
jscalzitti@reedbusiness.com

Why
You Should
Use This
Book

Why You'll Want to Use the Houston Home Book

At times, in this high-speed information-driven culture, we can easily become lost and disoriented. Where we find information, how we find it, and how credible this information is, has become critical to consumers everywhere.

The *Houston Home Book* recognizes and addresses these concerns, and provides ease of use and comfort to consumers looking to build, renovate or enhance their home. As a consumer, the anxiety of searching for trustworthy, experienced housing professionals can be overwhelming.

Relief is in Sight

The *Houston Home Book* puts an end to this stress. It offers you, the reader, a comprehensive, hands-on guide to building, remodeling, decorating, furnishing and landscaping a home in Houston. The book also offers readers convenience and comfort.

Convenience

The *Houston Home Book* compiles the area's top home service providers with easy-to-read listings by trade. It also dissuades readers' fears of unreliable service providers by featuring many of the finest professionals available, specialists who rank among the top 10 of their respective fields in Houston. Their outstanding work has netted them many awards in their fields. The other listings are recommendations made by these advertisers.

The goal of the *Houston Home Book* creators is to provide a high quality product that goes well beyond the scope of mere Yellow Pages. Its focus is to provide consumers with credible, reliable, and experienced professionals, accompanied by photographic examples of their work.

This crucial resource was unavailable to the founders of the *Houston Home Book* when they were working on their own home improvement projects. This lack of information spurred them on to create the book, and to assist other consumers in finding the proper professionals that suit their specific needs. Now, thanks to the team's entrepreneurial spirit, you have the *Houston Home Book* at your fingertips, to guide you on your home enhancement journey.

Comfort

Embrace this book, enjoy it and relish it, because at one time it didn't exist; but now, someone has done your homework for you. Instead of running all over town, you'll find in these pages:

• More than 700 listings of professionals, specializing in 40 different trades.

• An index listing these professionals by their specialty within their field.

• Instructional information for choosing and working with architects, contractors, landscapers and interior designers.

• More than 1,000 photos inspiring innovative interior and exterior modeling ideas.

Excitement...The Houston Home Book can turn your dream into a reality!

Joe Pisano, *Publisher*

The premier resource provider for the luxury home market

Houston Home Book

Contents

Continued

126

164

92D

193

178

143

About the Back Cover:
A mixture of influences, from the Classical age to the American Southwest, reside gracefully in this home by Hann Builders.

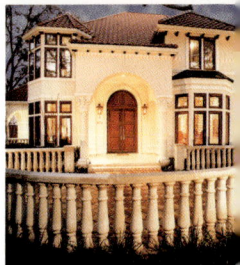

Contents

220B

83

148

114

24

How To Use

TABLE OF CONTENTS

Start here for an at-a-glance guide to the 11 tabbed categories and numerous subcategories. The book is organized for quick, easy access to the information you want, when you want it. The Table of Contents provides an introduction to the comprehensive selection of information.

DESIGN UPDATE

Read what top home industry professionals think are the most exciting new styles, future trends and best ideas in their fields as we continue into the millennium. See even more inspiring photos of some of the Houston area's most beautiful, up-to-date luxury homes and landscapes. It's a visual feast, full of great ideas.

"HOW-TO" ARTICLES

Each tabbed section begins with a locally researched article on how to achieve the best possible result in your home building, remodeling, decorating or landscape project. These pages help take the fear and trepidation out of the process. You'll receive the kind of information you need to communicate effectively with professionals and to be prepared for the nature of the process. Each article is a step-by-step guide, aiding you in finding the materials you need in the order you'll need them.

DESIGN EXCELLENCE AWARDS

Included are the results of our first annual Design Excellence Awards! Here you will find winning entries representing nearly every area of high-end, custom housing. From striking exteriors to awe-inspiring interiors, fabulous flooring to creative furniture designs, see who in your area is creating the most beautiful housing projects of our time. (Those who took the Gold went on to compete in the national event and Best Of Show. Read more about it in this section!)

This Book

DIVIDER TABS

Use the sturdy tabs to go directly to the section of the book you're interested in. A table of contents for each section's subcategories is printed on the front of each tab. Quick, easy, convenient.

LISTINGS

Culled from current, comprehensive data and qualified through careful local research, the listings are a valuable resource as you assemble the team of experts and top quality suppliers for your home project. We have included references to their ad pages throughout the book.

FEATURES!

We've devoted attention to specific areas within the various sections, such as Interior Design Spotlight. We've also gone in-depth, with feature articles in the Architects and Home Builders sections.

BEAUTIFUL VISUALS

The most beautiful, inspiring and comprehensive collections of homes and materials of distinction in Houston. On these pages, our advertisers present exceptional examples of their finest work. Use these visuals for ideas as well as resources.

INDEXES

This extensive cross reference system allows easy access to the information on the pages of the book. You can check by alphabetical order or individual profession.

The

A

THE 2003
HOME
BOOK
DESIGN
EXCELLENCE
AWARDS

THE ASHLEY GROU

Grou

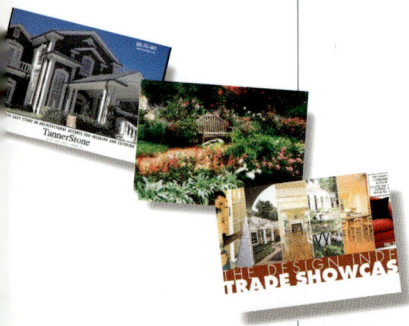

Design

*What are the hot ideas and attitudes that are shapin
where top local professionals tell what's happenin*

Photo by **Carl Mayfield**

Update

MANY LEVELS OF STYLE

Ironwood Custom Homes: "Our luxury home clients want stylish interiors and exteriors and they want that sense of style reflected in the smallest of details. The styling elements that are in high demand include arches, curves, ceiling treatments such as barrel vaults and exposed wood beams, and multi-depth elevations."

BATHS WITH CLASS

Designer Showcase: "Master baths with character as well as function have become important to luxury home owners. For instance, customized marble flooring and a domed bath may be paired with a crystal chandelier and hand–beaded, sheer draperies for a soft, romantic oasis. An additional level of elegance can be brought into the bath with such features as double mirrors, a bronze statue and a plush ottoman."

Photo by **Bruce Glass**

THE OUTDOOR LIVING ROOM

Pineloch Pool Construction: "More than ever before, backyards are becoming an extension of the home. By designing with this in mind, pool builders can create features not normally associated with a swimming pool and provide soothing water noise to accompany these elements. The incorporation of outdoor kitchens, fireplaces, firepits and lounging niches into the design of the swimming pool allows Houston homeowners to enjoy their yards year-round in a variety of ways."

THE HEART OF THE HOME

Hann Builders: "The kitchen is the most important space in most homes. No longer reserved for food preparation, kitchens have become the focal point of family life. No other room houses as much daily activity as the kitchen, so you want it to work well. At the same time, the kitchen is often a gathering place for parties, so you want it to be a showplace. Having a well designed kitchen that reflects your personality and lifestyle will have the most immediate and substantial impact on your quality of life."

Photo by **John Blackmer**

KID'S PLAY

Sport Court of Houston: "Since knowing where their children are playing is a growing concern for families everywhere, parents are having game courts installed in their backyards not only to provide the children with a place to play, but so that they can keep an eye on them at the same time. For the pleasure of the adults, putting greens are now being added to the list of backyard features growing in popularity."

BREAKING UP THE GRANITE

Rohe & Wright Builders: "**Our** clients are having a lot more fun with kitchen design. No longer do we see granite countertops in every home. Instead, clients are selecting honed slate, maple butcher block, or concrete countertops. Out with the tile backsplash as well. Now we install hammered copper, pressed tin, or thin brick for a backsplash look that stands out."

MAKING A STATEMENT

Elima Designs: "Attention to intricate details, to complete a design, establishes an individual and unique statement for each home. For instance, a custom designed embroidery for a window treatment and pillows can be hand drawn to correlate with a home's theme. The window treatments and pillows can then be embroidered in, say, silk thread on ultrasuede, to give a contrast of textures."

BACK TO BASICS

Watermark Homes: "I feel that the most exciting trend in custom home building is the movement back to basics, back to classical and more natural interiors. We see clients backing off from the opulent heavy moldings, and spending more emphasis on simplicity. Nonetheless, they are using quality materials to achieve a timeless, elegant appeal. Specialty cabinet and wall finishes are also popular, to achieve that Old World look. Less ceramic tile is being used, with more emphasis on natural stone. In general, then, the trends now call for greater simplicity, muted colors, timeless elegance, quality natural materials and homes that above all offer great comfort."

SURROUNDED WITH SOUND

Richard's Total Backyard Solutions: "The reason people add a spa to their backyard atmosphere is not only to relax in the warm water, but also to enjoy the hydromassage experience. Some of the new, unique technology like a Spaudio music system by Hot Springs allows you to actually feel the music. It sends sound waves through the spa shell, turning it into the speaker – surrounding your body with music."

OASIS UNDER THE RAINBOW

Platinum Pools: "There is so much happening in pool design and operation these days. Lighting the water has come a long way – homeowners can now select any number of colors of the rainbow to light the water. Lighting, along with the rest of the pool's operations, can now be controlled from within the home, with just the push of a single button. Around the water, the natural look is still the most popular style these days. Many clients like the oasis look, complete with waterfalls and lush rock formations."

SHADOWS AND LIGHT

Illuminations Lighting Design: "With increased attention on security concerns, outdoor lighting has come into focus as a primary deterrent to crime, theft and vandalism. Homeowners now realize security lighting can be achieved in an understated and elegant fashion with the application of moonshadow illumination. Moonshadow illumination is the placement of glare-free, mercury vapor lighting fixtures in the upper tree canopy directed through the foliage to create lighting with soft shadows. Mercury vapor is used due to the blue-green light, energy efficiency and long lamp life (24,000+ hours)."

THE AMBIANCE OF OLD

Eubanks Group Architects: "Capturing the charm and character found in older homes is a goal of many owners of new construction luxury homes. One strategy toward this goal is to integrate reclaimed materials or objects into the design of the new home. Antique objects such as stone mantels and windows, doors, light fixtures, hardware, tile and unique garden elements are combined to create the ambiance of the past while fitting the needs of the present."

OPENING UP, BRINGING EVERYONE IN

Smith Custom Builders, Inc.: "These days, most custom homes and remodels constructed have open concept designs, which lend themselves quite easily to gatherings of family and friends, leading to a real sense of closeness among all. Use of natural products like hardwoods, slate, marble and granite are popular choices among homeowners. Home automation systems are now a given in today's new homes, but considerations for current as well as future technologies are a must when these systems are installed."

GOD IS IN THE DETAILS

McVaugh Custom Homes, Inc.: "In today's custom homes, unique architectural designs and intricate details are becoming increasingly popular. Use of natural materials, stone columns, wrought iron detail, hardwoods, interior-stained cedar doors, butted glass windows and custom cabinetry make a big impact on the home, allowing it to stand apart from other residences in the area. These amenities are pure elegance, yet they still provide a warm and inviting setting for the homeowners and their guests."

FLOWING LANDSCAPES

Legacy Landscape Management, Inc.: "Homeowners look to their outdoor environments to be an extension of their homes, reflecting their individuality and taste. With a strong design, each element, including hardscape, plantscape, pools, drainage and irrigation can flow in harmony with the home. The attention to detail in the design is the cornerstone in achieving a dream garden."

THE 2002 HOME BOOK DESIGN EXCELLENCE AWARDS

A flight of fancy...
A dream beheld...
An open door....

Please join us in viewing Houston's winning entries in the first annual Home Book Design Excellence Award

Show, sponsored by The Ashley Group. In the following pages you will see numerous categories of winning entries representing nearly every area of high-end, custom housing. From striking exteriors to awe-inspiring interiors, from fabulous flooring to creative furniture designs,

37

you will see the most beautiful housing projects of our time created in Houston. The Home Book Design Excellence Award Show is both a regional and national event, with the gold winners in each category competing with gold winners in 21 other US markets. The results of

the national contest are revealed in the Best of the Best magazine. (More information on the Best of the Best can

be obtained at the end of this section.)

Gold

Winner: Eubanks Group Architects
Interior Designer: Stacy L. Graubart
Architect: Eubanks Group Architects
Contractor: Aspen Builders
Photographer: Fran Brennan

Silver

Winner: Eubanks Group Architects
Interior Designer: Marlys Tokerud
Architect: Eubanks Group Architects
Photographer: Filippo Castore

Bronze

Winner:
McVaugh Custom Homes, Inc.
Photographer: Rob Muir

Gold

Winner: Eubanks Group Architects
Interior Designer: Sophie Tomjanovich
Architect: Eubanks Group Architects
Contractor: Gerecht Builders
Photographer: Filippo Castore

Silver

Winner: Kent & Kent, Inc.
Interior Designer:
Bonnie Gustafson
Building Designer: Alan Kent
Contractor:
Karen Daugherty Homes
Photographer: Terry Halsey

Bronze

Winner: Guy M. Land Designer, Inc.
Designer: Guy Land
Contractor: Hallmark/Ruby
Photographer: Justin Patterson

Winner: Ironwood Homes
Interior Designer:
Christine White Designs
Architect: MSA of Houston
Contractor: Ironwood Homes
Photographer: Carl Mayfield

Gold

Silver

Winner:
Smith Custom Builders, Inc.
Architect: Kent & Kent, Inc.
Contractor:
Smith Custom Builders, Inc.
Photographer:
Century Publications

Bronze

Winner:
Smith Custom Builders, Inc.
Contractor:
Smith Custom Builders, Inc.
Photographer: Bruce Glass

Gold

Winner: Smith Custom Builders, Inc.
Architect: Kent & Kent, Inc.
Contractor: Smith Custom Builders, Inc.
Photographer: Century Publications

Remodeling Project

Gold

Winner: Smith Custom Builders, Inc.
Architect: Kent & Kent, Inc.
Contractor: Smith Custom Builders, Inc.
Photographer: Century Publications

Silver

Winner: Eubanks Group Architects
Interior Designer: Charles Faudree (Tulsa)
Architect: Eubanks Group Architects
Contractor: Crain Construction
Photographer: Filippo Castore

Gold

Winner: Classic Designs, Inc.
Interior Designer: Jana Erwin, ASID
Contractor: Mesa Verde Homes
Photographer: Rob Muir

Silver

Winner: Michael Easley Designs
Interior Designer:
Michael Easley, ASID
Photographer: Cindy Cady

Silver

Winner:
McVaugh Custom Homes, Inc.
Photographer: Rob Muir

Bronze

Winner:
McVaugh Custom Homes, Inc.
Photographer: Rob Muir

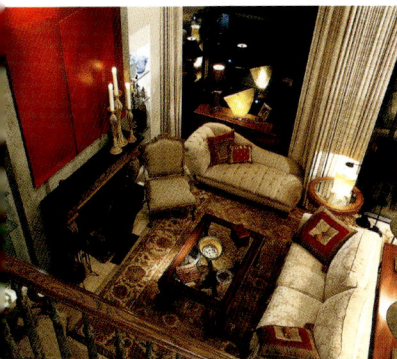

Honorable Mention

Winner: Source Design Studio
Interior Designer:
Richard Eastman
Photographer: Rex Spencer

Honorable Mention

Winner:
Susan Hanson Interior Design
Interior Designer:
Susan Hanson, ASID
Assistant Designer:
Randy Powers
Furniture: McGuire - Custom
Photographer: Phyllis Hand

Honorable Mention

Winner:
Guy M. Land Designer, Inc.
Designer: Guy Land
Contractor: Jerry Kirkpatrick
Photographer: Justin Patterson

Gold

Winner: Classic Designs, Inc.
Interior Designer: Jana Erwin, ASID
Contractor: Mesa Verde Homes
Photographer: Rob Muir

Gold

Winner: Susan Hanson Interior Design
Interior Designer: Susan Hanson
Assistant Designer: Randy Powers
Furniture: Kravet - Custom
Photographer: Phyllis Hand

Silver

Winner:
Susan Hanson Interior Design
Interior Designer: Susan Hanson
Assistant Designer: Louise Caster
Millwork/Cabinets/Stairs:
La Madera
Lighting: Horizon
Photographer: Rob Muir

Gold

Winner: Classic Designs, Inc.
Interior Designer: Jana Erwin, ASID
Contractor: Mesa Verde Homes
Photographer: Rob Muir

Gold   **Winner:** Exterior Worlds, Inc.

Silver

Winner: Smith Custom Builders, Inc.
Contractor: Smith Custom Builders, Inc.
Millwork/Cabinets/Stairs:
Douglas E. Smith
Photographer: Century Publications

Gold   **Winner:** Exterior Worlds, Inc.

Silver
Winner: Fox Family Pools

Gold

Winner: Fox Family Pools

Bronze

Winner: Fox Family Pools

Gold

Winner: Classic Designs, Inc.
Interior Designer: Jana Erwin, ASID
Contractor: Mesa Verde Homes
Kitchen & Bath Designer:
Jana Erwin, ASID
Photographer: Rob Muir

Gold

Winner: Kitchen & Bath Concepts
Interior Designer: Micqui McGowan
Kitchen & Bath Designer:
Micqui McGowan
Millwork/Cabinets/Stairs: Hillcraft
Photographer: Sharon Babbitt

Silver

Winner: Ironwood Homes
Millwork/Cabinets/Stairs:
Artisan Millworks
Photographer: Carl Mayfield

Bronze

Winner: Kitchen & Bath Concepts
Interior Designer: Micqui McGowan
Contractor: Talmadge Hargraves
Kitchen & Bath Designer:
Micqui McGowan
Cabinets: Wood Mode

Honorable Mention

Winner:
McVaugh Custom Homes, Inc.
Photographer: Rob Muir

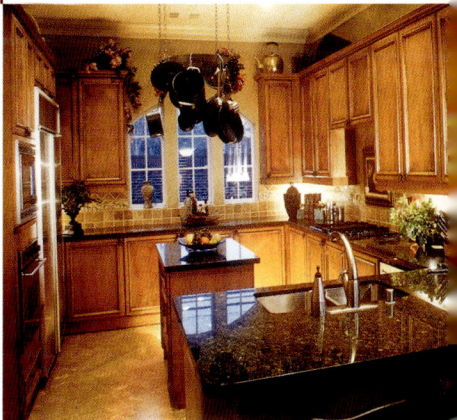

Gold

Winner: WM Shaw Associates, Inc.
Kitchen & Bath Designer: Bill Shaw
Stone/Tile/Marble: Walker Zanger
Lighting: M & M Lighting
Photographer: Jeff Necessary

Silver

Winner: Classic Designs, Inc.
Interior Designer: Jana Erwin, ASID
Contractor: Mesa Verde Homes
Kitchen & Bath Designer:
Jana Erwin, ASID
Photographer: Rob Muir

Silver

Winner:
McVaugh Custom Homes
Photographer: Rob Muir

Gold

Winner: Smith Custom Builders, Inc.
Architect: Kent & Kent, Inc.
Millwork/Cabinets/Stairs: Smith Custom Builders, Inc.
Photographer: Century Publications

Silver

Winner: Smith Custom Builders, Inc.
Architect: Kent & Kent, Inc.
Millwork/Cabinets/Stairs: Smith Custom Builders, Inc.
Photographer: Century Publications

Gold

Winner: Smith Custom Builders, Inc.
Architect: Kent & Kent, Inc.
Contractor: Smith Custom Builders, Inc.
Millwork/Cabinets/Stairs:
Smith Custom Builders, Inc.

Silver

Winner: Smith Custom Builders, Inc.

Winner: Classic Designs, Inc.
Interior Designer: Jana Erwin, ASID
Contractor: Mesa Verde Homes
Stone/Tile/Marble: Jana Erwin, ASID
Photographer: Rob Muir

Gold

Custom Furniture

Gold

Winner:
Gilani Collection Home Furnishings
Furniture: S. Shah Gilani, ASFD

Gold

Winner: Source Design Studio
Interior Designer: Richard Eastman
Photographer: Rex Spencer

Design Excellence Awards Judges

Hans Anderle is an Associate and Senior Designer with Bassenian/Lagoni Architects. He joined the award-winning Newport Beach, California firm in 1993. It is among the largest residential design firms involved in various high-quality projects across the United States and Asia.

Brian Brand, AIA, President of Baylis Architects in Bellevue, Washington, has been in the business for 30 years. His firm specializes in custom residential architecture projects, which have earned both local and national acclaim. Brian has served as a judge in numerous design competitions.

Karen Kitowski, ASID, has been in practice since 1963. She is Owner and Principle of Karen Kitowski & Company, Inc., located in San Francisco, California and Dallas, Texas. Her award-winning projects, ranging in states from Oregon to Texas, have not only been featured in local and national print, but on television as well.

Anthony Perry, AIA, Vice President of Orren Pickell Design Group, Bannockburn, Illinois, has served as a juror in several national design competitions. Perry has designed more than 250 homes in his 10 years with the firm, which under his leadership has been granted over 140 awards for architectural excellence.

Sandra L. Steiner, CKD, an ASID Allied and NKBA member, has been in the field 21 years and is President of Design at Steiner & Houck, Inc. in Columbia, Pennsylvania – a firm she started 10 years ago. Sandra's award-winning kitchen and bath designs are regularly featured in various national media.

Larry Yaw, FAIA, Principal of Cottle Graybeal Yaw Architects, has 28 years of professional experience and is a founding member of the firm, begun in 1970. In 1993 Larry was named into the FAIA due to his contributions to the standard of design and architectural innovations - the highest award granted by the American Institute of Architects.

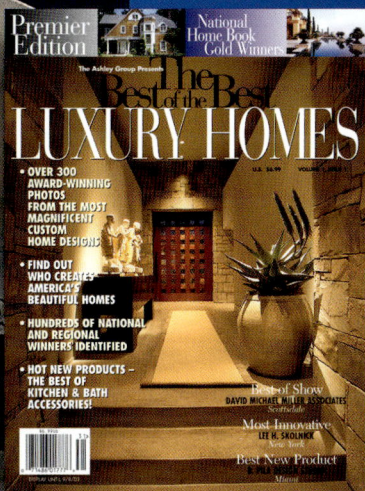

Houston's Premier
Home & Design
Sourcebook

The **Houston Home Book** is your final destination when searching for home remodeling, building and decorating resources. This comprehensive, hands-on sourcebook to building, remodeling, decorating, furnishing and landscaping a luxury home is required reading for the serious and discriminating homeowner. With more than 300 full-color, beautiful pages, the **Houston Home Book** is the most complete and well-organized reference to the home industry. This hardcover volume covers all aspects of the process, includes listings of hundreds of industry professionals, and is accompanied by informative and valuable editorial discussing the most recent trends. Ordering your copy of the **Houston Home Book** now can ensure that you have the blueprints to your dream home, in your hand, today.

Order your copy now!

**HOUSTON
HOME
BOOK**

Published by
The Ashley Group
10900 Northwest Freeway, Suite 122, Houston, TX 77092
713.263.0471 fax 713.263.1927
E-mail: ashleybooksales@reedbusiness.com

The 'Home' Team

61

Building a custom home is a team effort. The players on the team include the architect, the builder, the interior designer, a landscape architect and several trade contractors. It may be unclear, however, how the various team members work together and what they can do for the homeowner. We'll explain that and also flesh out the various roles of your home building roster.

SPOTLIGHT ON THE PLAYERS

Architect: A person trained and experienced in the design of buildings and the coordination and supervision of all aspect of the construction of buildings.

Builder: The individual or firm who is the employer of craftsmen required for erecting a building in accordance with the plans and specifications prepared by the architect and who carries the responsibility for doing so. Also called the General Contractor.

Interior Designer: A professionally space planner. Interior designers generate ideas for spaces that address the space's function and aesthetics. They select and specify a room's furnishings, fixtures, materials and colors, and monitor the construction and installation of the design. In some states these professionals must be certified.

Landscape Architect: Landscape architects plan the layout of "hardscape" (such as walkways, retaining walls, sculptures, and fountains) as well as "softscape" (soil, grass, plants, and trees). A landscape architect may work with architects, surveyors, and engineers to identify an optimal arrangement for site development. He or she will create detailed reports, sketches, models, construction diagrams, and cost estimates for your project.

Landscape Contractor: A trained builder or installer of landscapes, retained to implement the plans of landscape architects.

ASSEMBLING THE TEAM

Once you've made the decision to build your custom home, you should pull your team together as soon as possible. Having all the team members assembled at the same time will do wonders for the communication between them. And when the members of your team are communicating, the project will go more smoothly, it's more likely to stay on schedule and on budget, and the likelihood of some unwelcome surprises popping up are greatly reduced.

In the traditional approach, the homeowner and architect may simply execute their dream lists in the home's design and put the finished concept out to four or five contractors to bid. Unless an architect is especially adept at knowing building costs, this can be a risky approach. For a $1.5 million home, for

---

OTHER POTENTIAL TEAM PLAYERS:

Design/Build General Contractor: **A builder who assumes overall responsibility for designing and executing a project, as opposed to having an independent architect draft the plans and a general contractor execute them.**

Design/Build Landscape Firm: **A company that offers its clients both the design of the project and the services to construct it. It differs from firms that may just offer the design or the construction services.**

Structural Engineer: **A person degreed in that branch of engineering concerned with the design and construction of structures to withstand physical forces or displacements without danger of collapse or without loss of serviceability or function.**

Residential Designer: **A home designer who is not a licensed architect. Residential design is for the most part exempt from state laws that regulate the**

practice of architecture, and so does not require the services of a licensed architect.

Landscape Designer: A landscape designer uses a knowledge of horticulture to select plants and flowers and direct their placement. While landscape designers often pursue a university course of study such as horticulture, there is no standard certification process in the U.S. for them.

Certified Kitchen and Bath Designer: Certified Kitchen Designers (CKDs) and Certified Bathroom Designers (CBDs) are a select group of expert designers who specialize in the design, planning, and execution of kitchens, bathrooms, and other built-in units for your home.

Interior Decorator: A decorator works with surface decoration – paint, fabric, furnishings, lighting and other materials. Because no license is required, upholsterers, housepainters, and other trades people also claim the title "decorator."

example, an architect's fee of $100K, or 6 to 7 percent, is typical, so this fee is already a sunken cost, and if the home is too expensive to build, additional architectural costs must be incurred to modify the design.

In the construction management approach, a construction manager (usually the general contractor or his employee) will be brought in to do a budget at three stages in the design process: when 20% of the architects drawings are completed, when 80% are completed, and when 100% are completed. In this approach, the costs are evaluated at each stage, and adjustments concerning materials and services are made if the project appears to be over budget. The client may be happy with the final product, but it may not be the project he or she envisioned in the beginning.

Interior designers say that, ideally, they should be brought on board at the time the architect is developing the basic scheme of the house. If your interior designer is involved early on in your project, he or she can give input to the architect and both can collaborate with the contractor – as to what materials would or wouldn't be appropriate for what

the others want to do, for example. All three can proceed with a better understanding of what each are doing.

Your landscape architect will need to be part of your assembled team before any actual digging or planting takes place. In that way, if there are drainage or soil concerns that need to be addressed, those issues can be dealt with by the team, and any obstacles they present can be minimized. This early and open communication also insures that their plans would not affect any other part of your home's design; for instance, a builder may want trees kept a certain distance from the home, to allow for better exterior air circulation.

In certain cases, a team member may be good at putting home building teams together. Sometimes a real estate broker who is assisting in site selection may take the lead in assembling the team. In other cases, it may fall to the architect or the builder. As general contractor, the builder contracts directly with the trade contractors. Because of this contractual relationship, the builder assumes the risks of construction. For example, if the trade contractor goes bankrupt, the builder assumes the trade contractor's liabilities for the job. Interior designers, even if they are recommended to a homeowner by a builder or architect, encourage an initial meeting with clients, so that the designer and client develop a unified vision of the home and an understanding of each other.

TEAM INTERACTIONS

Architect & Landscaper

Clients often have a location already chosen for their custom home, and usually have a favorite spot on the site, such as a hilltop or an area with a site line to a lake or an ocean. The landscape architect can provide valuable insight to help the architect enhance those sites. For example, during the initial site visits, the landscape architect can help the architect judge the feasibility of moving earth to alter the grades the home may reside on, or provide input as to the costs of placing a disappearing-edge pool on the site. In the end, you are the beneficiary of a cohesive vision of your dream home.

Architect & Builder

Architects and builders often work side by side. Usually they are familiar with each other's work and method of working. Especially in cases where the homeowner hires either the architect or the builder,

and one professional hires the other, they have a history of working together and know what to expect. The builder won't try to make design decisions, and the architect won't try to tell the builder how to execute the plan.

The architect can conduct site studies, help secure planning and zoning approvals, and perform a variety of other pre-design tasks. In most cases in upscale home building, a client will already own a favorite site. At this point the owner will bring in the team to achieve the vision of a dream home.

Typically, a homeowner will sit down with an architect and go over concept drawings during the design stage. Today's modern tools of computer-aided-design (CAD) software enable owners to see the impact of design decisions almost immediately. This can significantly cut down the time needed for the conception stage.

During the second stage, once the concept of the home is established, preliminary drawings will be created. At this stage the builder is usually brought in, especially as cost considerations are usually addressed at this time. If the homeowner isn't willing to foot the bill, there is no sense in going down a design road that may involve significant costs. The builder will provide a range within which he'll be able to achieve the design goals. Since the architect and builder are usually familiar with each other's work, typically these cost figures are accurate and can be trusted.

TOTAL CONSTRUCTION COSTS VS. TOTAL PROJECT COST

Prepare yourself for expenses that go above and beyond that of the cost of your home and the fees of the primary professionals working on your project. On top of the construction cost, you should be aware that you may be paying as much as another 25 percent in "soft costs."
These include:
• **Sales Tax**
• **Fees:**
  Architect
  Structural
  Engineer
  Surveyor
  Interior Design
  Consult
  Soil Engineer

This does not include the cost of the land.
   Also, in newer areas, there are "Impact

In the next stage, construction documents are finalized, and the architect registers the documents with the local municipality. At this stage a builder will contact the trade contractors best suited to the project. The job may not always go to the lowest bidder, however, as the general contractor may realize that certain trade contractors may have a reputation for reliability and quality, justifying their higher price.

Once building begins, the architect is required to make site visits to the worksite, to ensure that building is progressing according to plan. If not, he

Fees." These are city fees for fire, police, city infrastructure, schools, etc. Homeowners should find out if there are any "assessments" due.

will instruct the contractor to correct the work that is being done, or to undo and start over any errant work, if necessary.

Architect, Builder & Interior Designer

At times, an architect may simply design the shell of a house, and an interior designer will be brought in to finish some of the rooms (designers are trained to complete the design of non load-bearing structures such as staircases, fireplaces, etc.).Your interior designer will work with you to select all of the interior architectural finishes, tile, millwork and furnishings inside the home. After you have made your decisions of what to do with the space and what to bring into it, the designer will get together with your architect and contractor to discuss these things. The architect and contractor will let the designer know if everything you've decided on can be done, how it can be done, and if it what you want falls within your pre-determined budget.

There are some interior designers who take great pride in their talents when it comes to custom kitchen and bath projects. You may choose to work solely with your interior designer on a custom kitchen and bath project, or the designer may bring in a kitchen and bath designer. Regardless of whom you choose to design your kitchen and bath, consultation with one of these design professionals is highly recommended before you embark on such a project.

With this integrated team approach, everything is discussed before any action is taken, and none of the professionals working on your home, or you, for that matter, are left in the dark. ■

ARCHITECTURE

& DESIGN

"Our goal is to positively affect people's lives through creating unique and inspiring places for living."

Russell King, AIA

KING RESIDENTIAL GROUP INC.

ARCHITECTURE   INTERIOR

www.krgi.net

tel. 713.520.5220

1971 West Gray, Houston, Texas 77019

DESIGN   DESIGN/BUILD

69

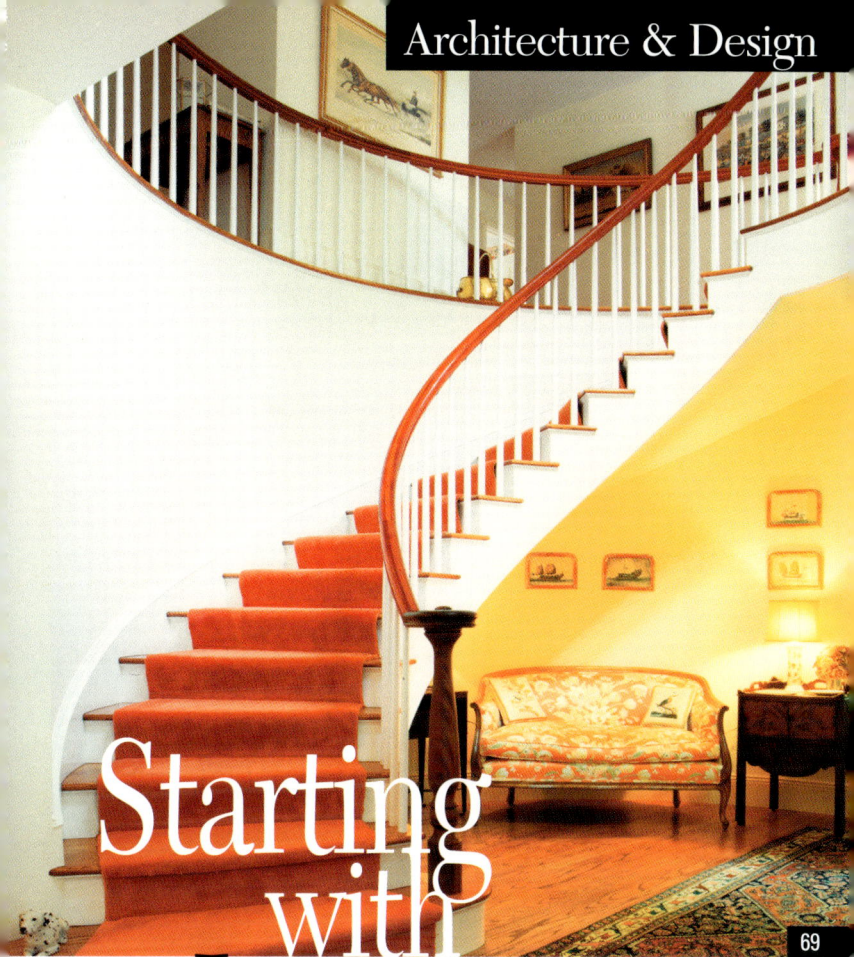

Starting with Inspiration

What do people think about when they hire architects to design their homes? Some have heard of the lofty reputation of an architect. They believe to have the best home, the best professional must design it. Some homeowners, on the other hand, leave the decision up to the builder, and trust the builder to choose the architect who is right for the homeowner. The most important concern, however, should be the realization of the homeowner's vision. The architect who listens, whose designs satisfy and inspire, is the architect for you.

An architect will oversee the entire homebuilding process, and will ensure that your home is constructed according to plan and on budget. He or she can see living space and utilization where others see only walls and impediments. Your architect can make your home more energy-efficient, or help you restore a home to its former charm and grandeur. Let us introduce you to the area's finest architects and residential designers, those talented creators of dreams.

YOUR OWN DREAM TEAM

Whether you're building your dream home in the city, a second vacation home, or remodeling your home in the suburbs, it takes a team to design and build a high quality residential project. A team of an architect, builder, interior designer, kitchen and bath designer, and landscape architect/designer should be assembled very early in the process. When these five professionals have the opportunity to collaborate before ground is broken, you'll reap the rewards for years to come. Their blend of experience and ideas can give you insights into the fabulous possibilities of your home and site you never considered. Their association will surely save you time, money and eventually frustration.

THE ARCHITECT – MAKING THE DREAM REAL

Licensed architects provide three basic, easily defined tasks. First, they design, taking into account budget, site, owner's needs and existing house style. Second, they produce the necessary technical drawings and specifications to accomplish the desires of their clients, and explain to a contractor in adequate detail what work needs to be done. Lastly, architects participate in the construction process. This straightforward mission requires more than education.

It requires listening. The best architects have gained their status by giving their clients exactly what they want – even when those clients have difficulty articulating what that is. How? By creatively interpreting word pictures into real pictures. By eliciting the spirit of the project and following that spirit responsibly as they develop an unparalleled design.

It requires experience. Significant architects, such as those included in your Home Book, maintain a reputation for superiority because their buildings are stunningly conceived, properly designed and technically sound. If a unique, steeply pitched roof was custom-designed for you by a licensed architect with an established reputation, you can be confident that it is buildable.

Suggestions by an experienced architect can add value and interest to your new home or remodeling project. He or she may suggest you wire your home for the technology of the future, frame up an attic for future use as a second floor, or build your countertops at varying levels to accommodate people of different heights.

This area is blessed with many talented architects. It's not uncommon for any number of them to be working on a luxury vacation retreat in another country

WHY YOU SHOULD WORK WITH A TOP ARCHITECT

1. They are expert problem solvers. A talented architect can create solutions to your design problems, and solve the problems that stand in the way of achieving your dream.

2. They have creative ideas. You may see a two-story addition strictly in terms of its function - a great room with a master suite upstairs. An architect immediately applies a creative eye to the possibilities.

3. They provide a priceless product and service. A popular misconception about architects is that their fees make their services an extravagance. In reality, an architect's fee represents a small percentage of the overall building cost.

or a unique second home in another state. Their vision and devotion to design set a standard of excellence for dynamic and uncompromising quality.

WORKING WITH AN ARCHITECT

The best relationships are characterized by close collaborative communication. The architect is the person you're relying on to take your ideas, elevate them to the highest level, and bring them to life in a custom design that's never been built before. So take your time in selecting the architect. It's not unusual for clients to spend two or three months interviewing prospective architects.

In preparation for the interview process, spend time fine-tuning your ideas. Put together an Idea Notebook (See the sidebar 'Compile an Idea Notebook'). Make a wish list that includes every absolute requirement and every fantasy you've ever wanted in a home. Visit builders' models to discover what 3,000 sq. ft. looks like in comparison to 6,000 sq. ft., how volume ceilings impact you or what loft living feels like. Look at established and new neighborhoods to get ideas about the relationship between landscaping and homes, and what level of landscaping you want.

GOOD COMMUNICATION SETS THE TONE

The first meeting is the time to communicate all of your desires for your new home or remodeling project, from the abstract to the concrete. You're creating something new, so be creative in imprinting your spirit and personality on the project. Be bold in expressing your ideas, even if they are not fully developed or seem unrealistic. Share your Idea Notebook and allow the architect to keep it as plans are being developed. Be prepared to talk about your lifestyle, because the architect will be trying to soak up as much information about you and your wishes as possible.

• Be frank about your budget. Although some clients are unrestricted by budgetary concerns, most must put some control on costs, and good architects expect and respect this. Great ideas can be achieved on a budget, and the architect will tell you what can be achieved for your budget.

• However, sticking to your budget requires tremendous self-discipline. If there's a luxury you really want, (a second laundry room, a built-in aquarium) it's probably just as practical to build it into your design from the outset, instead of paying for it in a change order once building has begun.

WHAT'S YOUR LIFESTYLE?

(Your architect will want to know.)
• Who lives in your house now?
• Who will live there in the future?
• Who visits and for how long?
• Do you like traditional, contemporary or eclectic design?
• Why are you moving or remodeling?
• What aspects of your current home need to be improved upon?
• Do you like functional, minimalist design, or embellishments and lots of style?
• Do you entertain formally or informally?
• How much time will you spend in the master bedroom? Is it spent reading, watching TV, working or exercising?
• What are the primary functions of the kitchen?
• Do you need a home office?
• Do you like lots of open space or little nooks and crannies?
• What kind of storage do you need?

71

AMERICAN
INSTITUTE OF
ARCHITECTS

**1735 New York
Ave., NW
Washington, DC
20006
800.AIA.3837
Fax:
202.626.7547
www.aia.org**

AIA is a professional association of licensed architects, with a strong commitment to educating and serving the general public. It frequently sponsors free seminars called, "Working with an Architect," which feature local architects speaking on home design and building. AIA has also produced an educational package including a video entitled, "Investing in a Dream," and a brochure, "You and Your Architect." It's available at many local libraries throughout the area.

74

Think practically. Consider what you don't like about your current home. If noise from the dishwasher bothers you at night, tell your architect you want a quiet bedroom, and a quiet dishwasher. Think about the nature of your future needs. Architects note that their clients are beginning to ask for "barrier-free" and ergonomic designs for more comfortable living as they age or as their parents move in with them.

A key role architects can play is in the planning for a secure home. Your architect can perform a security assessment, which will determine what is to be protected, what is the risk level and nature of the potential threat, what are the property's vulnerabilities, and what can be done to achieve the desired level of protection.

BUILDING BEGINS: BIDDING AND NEGOTIATION

If your contract includes it, your architect will bid your project to contractors he or she considers appropriate for your project, and any contractor you wish to consider. You may want to include a contractor to provide a "control" bid. If you wish to hire a specific contractor, you needn't go through the bidding process, unless you're simply curious about the range of responses you may receive. After the architect has analyzed the bids and the field is narrowed, you will want to meet the contractors to see if you're compatible, if you're able to communicate clearly, and if you sense a genuine interest in your project. These meetings can take place as a contractor walks through a home to be remodeled, or on a tour of a previously built project if you're building a new home.

If your plans come in over budget, the architect is responsible for bringing the costs down, except, of course, if the excess is caused by some item the architect had previously cautioned you would be prohibitive.

Not all people select an architect first. It's not uncommon for the builder to help in the selection of an architect, or for a builder to offer "design/build" services with architects on staff, just as an architectural firm may have interior designers on staff. ■

"Our goal is to positively affect people's lives through creating unique and inspiring places for living."

Russell King, AIA

KING RESIDENTIAL GROUP INC.

ARCHITECTURE • DESIGN BUILD • INTERIOR DESIGN

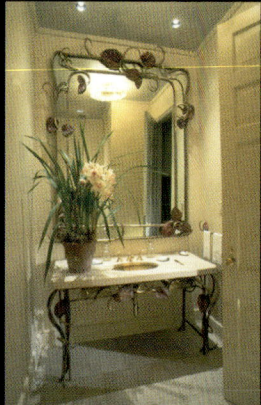

EGA

EUBANKS GROUP ARCHITECTS

ARCHITECTURE

URBAN PLANNING

Galveston's Historic Pleasure Pier & Hotel

INTERIOR DESIGN

ARCHITECTURAL ANTIQUES AND FURNISHINGS

3202 ARGONNE ST. HOUSTON, TEXAS 77098
TEL: (713) 522-2652 - FAX: (713) 522-2653

2328 BALL ST. GALVESTON, TEXAS 77550
TEL: (409) 621-1900 - FAX: (409) 621-1999

790 S. CASTELL AVE. NEW BRAUNFELS, TX 78130
TEL: (830) 625-2652 - FAX: (830) 625-2654

WWW.EUBANKS-ARCHITECTS.COM

ARCHITECTURAL SOLUTIONS, INC.

5858 Westheimer Rd., Suite 310, Houston, TX. 77057
Phone: 713-978-6989 Fax: 713-978-7085
www.asi-design.com

Entertaining and relaxing beyond interior walls
has challenged today's architects to create outdoor
living areas with strong architectural detailing
and stimulating design.

Photo courtesy of **Kent & Kent, Inc.**

Archit

DESIGNS
FOR LIVING

"C lients are spending a good amount of time considering how to customize their homes to suit their family's needs," said Ed Eubanks, president, Eubanks Group Architects. "The results are more unique opportunities for us to create truly exciting living spaces." As you'll see, Houston area architects and residential designers are up to the challenge of creating magnificent homes to live in, grow with and expand upon.

ecture

Hand-crafted detailing and exquisite design accompany today's most luxurious wine rooms.

Photo courtesy of **Eubanks Group Architects**

Archit

This contemporary seaside home's spectacular views and abundant natural light are achieved through the positioning of generous windows of various sizes and shapes.

The Great Outdoors

No longer simply patio chairs and umbrellas, today's outdoor living areas are an extension of the home in more ways than one. As entertainment destinations, cozy family rooms and exquisite kitchens, they're used on a daily basis.

"Generally, I speak with my clients about how many people they want to accommodate," said residential building designer Kevin Young, president, Kevin Young Designers, Inc. "Sometimes they want an area just large enough for the family, and other times they're looking for a true entertainment area, where they can sit 12 or more guests down for an elaborate dinner." Young added that gaining this information from a client allows them to design a room with the perfect dimensions and amenities for their needs. From the full line of kitchen appliances, fireplaces and casual furniture you would most likely see in the average family room, outdoor living in Houston has taken on a new look.

Conveniently Comfortable

It's not easy to make good use of these outdoor living rooms in southern Texas. Summers are downright hot, making even a dip in the pool an uncomfortable experience. But architects and designers are putting Mother Nature's challenges to rest with the help of modern technology. No longer are air-conditioning systems cooling just the insides of homes, you'll find

ecture

Outdoor rooms need a stunning view. With that in mind, many architects position the rooms beside the pool and spa area, with a view of the golf course or with direct access to the lake.

them outdoors as well. Ceiling fans combined with air conditioning systems make for a very pleasant and energy efficient outdoor area.

Soaring temperatures and high humidity levels aren't the only concerns of homeowners when considering the addition of an outdoor living space. "We install permanent screens in these areas to deter flies and mosquitoes," said Young. Unfortunately, screened-in areas tend to darken the interior of the home, so the happy median has resulted in the installation of an insect repellent system in the overhang of the home. Built-

Today's kitchens are more than just a place to prepare the evening meal. Homeowners want a unique atmosphere with enhanced detailing, ornate materials and a feeling of personality.

in nozzles spray a mist of insecticide to help eliminate pests. This pricey option is safe for humans and pets, and only takes a few seconds to get the job done for the remainder of the day.

Cheers!

Entertaining inside the home has changed as well with the addition of elaborate wine cellars and tasting rooms. This space has become more than just a temperature controlled storage area, it's a place to spend time in and entertain friends. Passionate collectors often include a tasting bar or small bistro table and chairs in their wine cellars. "In a recent project we used a stone wall fountain as a sink," said Eubanks. In another project, a dungeon door from France with five large slide bolts and locks was used as entry into the space. These rooms are not just for entertaining, they're great conversation pieces.

You won't find all wine rooms in a dungeon-like atmosphere. Many homeowners are moving the rooms upstairs, off the kitchen or dining room to create a focal point. "We'll use glass doors or iron gates to create a stunning entrance. We've even done an entire dining room wall in stone arches where the wine racks were set in. We'll use stone on the floor and brick on the ceiling to make the dining room feel like an Old World wine cellar," said Kevin Young.

ecture

A cozy sitting area provides the family chef an opportunity to converse with guests during meal preparation.

Photo courtesy of **Eubanks Group Architects**

Finding Function

Just as dining rooms have taken on a new appearance, many traditionally formal gathering areas of the home have been reinvented. Living rooms and traditional entertaining areas have been replaced by an open floor plan that's more family friendly. Residential designer Alan Kent, president, Kent & Kent, Inc. says many families are creating study nooks just off the kitchen, complete with computers. This allows parents to prepare dinner and help their children with homework. Kent's also noticed a surge in the number of parents who home school their children. "We're creating swing rooms in many of our homes. These rooms are being used as classrooms, complete with bathrooms. This allows parents to teach their children and be separate from the rest of the home." Kent says once the children have left the home, this room takes on a new life as a guest or in-law suite, or may even become the master bedroom as the homeowner ages. "Clients are helping us design homes that are functional for their growing family and will continue to be functional as they age."

Archit

It's evident today's homeowner is looking for better ways to utilize space. For Alan Kent, this meant designing a kitchen that was also a functioning art gallery. "She [the client] wanted a kitchen without cabinets above the countertops so the space was free to display her art collection." The kitchen area also acts as a sitting room and breakfast area, complete with casual furniture, a television and computer desk. "It's a room she truly lives in and puts to good use and the design reflects that," said Kent.

Ed Eubanks sees an increase in a more conversation friendly kitchen, making for the perfect space for interesting architectural detailing. As the hub of any social gathering, Eubanks feels it's important to use interesting materials when creating the kitchen design. This may mean antique and reclaimed stone, old light fixtures, heavy wood doors or vaulted ceilings clad in brick or stone. Combine this Old World character with new stainless steel appliances and you have warmth and comfort your guests can respond to.

Whether it's a kitchen, outdoor living room or custom wine cellar, creative minds, charming details and a sense of adventure can make your dream home a reality. ■

Large, open rooms with vaulted ceilings provide the perfect backdrop for entertaining large groups of friends and family.

Photo courtesy of **Eubanks Group Architects**

ecture

Architecture
& Design

ARCHITECTURAL SOLUTIONS, INC.... ....**(713) 978-6989**
    5858 Westheimer Rd., Suite 310, Houston   Fax:(713) 978-7085
    See ad on page 78, 79
    <u>Website:</u> www.asi-design.com

EUBANKS GROUP ARCHITECTS ....**(713) 522-2652**
    3202 Argonne Street, Houston   Fax:(713) 522-2653
    See ad on page 76, 77
    <u>Website:</u> www.eubanks-architects.com
    <u>e-mail:</u> ega@eubanks-architects.com

HARRELL ARCHITECTS, INC.... ....**(713) 722-7071**
    9601 Katy Freeway, Suite 270, Houston   Fax:(713) 722-7072
    See ad on page 68D
    <u>Website:</u> www.harrellarchitects.com
    <u>e-mail:</u> pharrell@harrellarchitects.com

KING RESIDENTIAL GROUP, INC.... ....**(713) 520-5220**
    1971 West Gray, Houston   Fax:(713) 520-5233
    See ad on page 68B, 68C, 75
    <u>Website:</u> www.krgi.net
    <u>e-mail:</u> rking@krgi.net

Residential
Designers

KENT & KENT INC ....**(713) 977-0777**
    2900 Wilcrest, Suite 120, Houston   Fax:(713) 977-0778
    See ad on page 89
    <u>e-mail:</u> kentdsgn@ev1.net

KEVIN YOUNG DESIGNER, INC ....**(713) 956-1491**
    4411 Dacoma St., Houston   Fax:(713) 957-4656
    See ad on page 90, 91
    <u>Website:</u> www.kyd.com
    <u>e-mail:</u> kyoung@kyd.com

Live Within Your Means...

KEVIN YOUNG
DESIGNERS, INC.

713.956.1491

kyoung@kyd.com
www.kyd.com

Photography by John Blackmer

Beyond Your Dreams

ARCHITECTURE

Architect
An individual experienced in architectural design, process and construction. He or she is licensed by the state and must spend 5 to 8 years studying architecture in college and a minimum of 2 to 3 years as an apprentice to an architect before taking the Architectural Registration Exam.

Arts & Crafts Movement
A functional style of architecture and dècor that began in the mid 19th century in response to the excesses of the Victorian Age.

Federal style
A post-colonial American style from about 1780 to 1820. This style is usually characterized by a symmetrical façade with a giant entrance portico, common brick construction or clapboard over timber framing with corner boards and exterior fireplaces at either end of the building.

Georgian Style
Popular in England during the reigns of King George I to the IV, this house style emerged in the United States between 1700 and 1780. It consists of two to three stories, is large and formal with a rectangular plan and symmetrical wings and a stone or brick façade.

Louis XIV, Louis Quatorze style
What is known as the Baroque style in France in its early years consisted of heavy-handed and grandiose decoration, as well as strictly symmetrical style. Developed during the high classical period under the rule of Louis XIV (1643-1715), this style culminated in the building of Versailles.

Louis XV, Louis Quinze style
Also known as Rococco, this is a lighter style that is by definition asymmetrical and fanciful – developed during Louis XV's rule in France (1715-1774).

Louis XVI, Louis Seize style
Also called Neoclassicism, this style goes back to classical symmetry and taut outlines and is characterized by its austerity. This style came about during the rule of Louis XVI (1774-1792) and ended with the French Revolution.

Mansard roof
A roof having a double slope on all four sides, the lower slope being much steeper.

Spanish Colonial Revival Style
An eclectic style based loosely on one or more phases of Spanish Colonial architecture; most common from about 1915 to the present. Buildings in this style usually have a façade with unadorned stucco or plastered walls; glazed and/or unglazed wall tiles; a covered porch or arcade; a patio; wrought-iron balconies or balconets; round arches over the most prominent windows and heavy wood doors, often elaborately paneled or carved.

CUSTOM
HOME BUILDING
&
REMODELING

Getting It Done

Every great plan is only as good as the professionals who execute it. By choosing a builder with a background in creating your type of home, you will go a long way toward making the home building process – which may take a year or two depending on the breadth of your vision – a smooth one. Your builder will bring technical skill in construction, knowledge of materials and finishes, and expertise in managing projects to the building of your home. The builder, or general contractor, knows the best craftsmen for the job, and will work closely with the architect to make your dream a reality.

It is essential to choose a company or individual with whom you and the architect can establish a good rapport. A candid exchange of ideas, with the requisite caveats against going over budget or planning areas that are difficult to execute, will make for a healthy and successful working relationship. A relationship that will help create a beautiful home.

Photo courtesy of **Allegro Builders**

WHICH COMES FIRST – THE ARCHITECT OR THE BUILDER?

Answering this question can seem like the "chicken or the egg" riddle: Do you hire the builder first, the architect first, or choose a design/build firm, where both functions are under the same roof?

If you work first with an architect, his or her firm will recommend builders they know have a track record in building homes of the same caliber you desire. Most likely, your architect contract will include bidding and negotiation services with these builders, and you may expect help in analyzing bids and making your selection. Your architect contract also may include construction administration, in which the architect makes site visits to observe construction, review the builder's applications for payment, and help make sure the home is built according to the plans.

Perhaps you've seen previous work or know satisfied clients of a custom home builder, and wish to work with him. In this scenario, the builder will recommend architects who are experienced in successfully designing homes and/or additions similar to what you want. The builder will support you, and the architect will cost-control information through realistic cost figures, before products are integrated into the house.

If you like the idea of working with one firm for both the architectural design and building, consider a design/build firm. Design/build firms offer an arrangement that can improve time management and efficient communication, simply by virtue of having both professional functions under the same roof. There is also added flexibility as the project develops. If you decide you want to add a feature, the design/build firm handles the design process and communicates the changes internally to the builder. When you interview a design/builder firm, it's important to ascertain that the firm has a strong architectural background, with experienced custom home architects on staff.

All scenarios work and no one way is always better than the other. Make your choice by finding professionals you trust and with whom you feel comfortable. Look for vision and integrity and let the creative process begin.

FINDING THE RIGHT CHEMISTRY

The selection of a builder or remodeler is a major decision, and should be approached in a thoughtful, unhurried manner. Allow plenty of time to interview and research at least two candidates before making your choice. Hours invested at this point can save months of time later on.

TEN GOOD
QUESTIONS
TO ASK A
BUILDER'S
PAST
CLIENTS

1. Are you happy with your home?
2. Was the house built on schedule?
3. Did the builder respect the budget and give an honest appraisal of costs early on?
4. Did the builder bring creativity to your project?
5. Were you well informed so you properly understood each phase of the project?
6. Was the builder accessible and on-site?
7. Does the builder provide good service now that the project is complete?
8. How much help did you get from the builder in choosing the products in your home?
9. Is the house well built?
10. Would you hire the builder again?

At the initial interview, the most important information you'll get is not from brochures, portfolios, or a sales pitch, but from your own intuition. Ask yourself: Can we trust this person to execute plans for our dream home, likely the biggest expenditure of our lifetime? Is there a natural two-way communication, mutual respect, and creative energy? Does he have the vision to make our home unique and important? Is his sense of the project similar to ours? Will we have any fun together? Can we work together for at least a year?

If you answer "Yes!" you've found the most valuable asset – the right chemistry.

CHECK REFERENCES, GET INVOLVED

The most distinguished builders in the area expect, even want, you to check their references. More luxury home clients are taking the time to do this research as the move toward quality workmanship continues to grow.

Talk to clients. Get a list of clients spanning the last three to five years, some of whom are owners of projects similar to yours. Call them and go visit their homes or building sites. Satisfied customers are only too happy to show you around and praise the builder who did the work. If you can, speak with a past client not on the builder's referral list. Finding one unhappy customer is not cause for concern, but if you unearth a number of them, cross that builder off your list.

Visit a construction site. Clients who get the best results appreciate the importance of the sub-contractors. Their commitment to quality is at the heart of the job. Do the subcontractors appear to be professional? Are they taking their time in doing their work? Is the site clean and neat?

Contact trade contractors with whom the builder has worked. If they vouch for the builder's integrity and ability, you'll know the firm has earned a good professional reputation. Meeting trade contractors also provides a good measure for the quality of workmanship you'll receive.

Visit the builder's office. Is it well-staffed and organized? Does this person offer the technology for virtual walk-throughs? Do you feel welcome there?

Find out how long the builder has been in business. Experienced custom builders have strong relationships with top quality trade contractors and architects, a comprehensive knowledge of products and materials, and skills to provide the best service before, during and after construction.

Ask how many homes are currently being built and how your project will be serviced. Some builders work on several homes at once; some limit their total to 10 or 12 a year.

CAN YOU TELL THE DIFFERENCE?

Manufactured stone (also called cast stone, since the product is poured into molds in a liquid form) can provide the same look and feel of natural stone. In some instances, such as in driveways and walkways, manufactured stone or concrete cast in the shape of say, cobblestone, can be the better alternative, due to its uniformity. Natural stone shapes have to be cut and carved by hand, which involves a great deal of labor and expense. The price of cast stone varies depending on the style and level of detail, but it generally costs about half as much as natural products.

95

LAYING A FOUNDATION FOR SUCCESS

Two documents, the contract and the timeline, define your building experience. The contract lays down the requirements of the relationship and the timeline delineates the order in which the work is done. While the contract is negotiated once at the beginning of the relationship, the timeline continues to be updated and revised as the project develops.

THE CONTRACT

The American Institute of Architects (AIA) provides a standard neutral contract which is widely used in the area, but some firms write their own contracts. As with any contract, get legal advice, read carefully, and assume nothing. If landscaping is not mentioned, then landscaping will not be provided. Pay careful attention to:

• Payment schedules. When and how does the builder get paid? How much is the deposit (depends on the total cost of the project but $10,000 to $25,000 is not uncommon) and will it be applied against the first phase of the work? Do you have the right to withhold any payment until your punch list is completed? Will you write checks to the builder (if so, insist on sworn waivers) or only to the title company? Remodeling contracts typically use a payment schedule broken into thirds – one-third up front, one-third half-way through the project, and one-third at completion. You may withhold a negotiated percentage of the contract price until you're satisfied that the terms of the contract have been met and the work has been inspected. This should be stipulated in the contract. Ten percent is the average amount to be held back, but is negotiable based on the overall size of the project.

Builders and remodeling specialists who attract a quality-minded, high-end custom home client are contacted by institutions offering attractive construction or bridge and end loan packages. Ask your contractor for referrals if you want to do some comparative shopping.

• The total cost – breakdown of labor and materials expenses.

• Change order procedures. Change orders on the average add seven to 10 percent to the cost of a custom home. Be clear on how these orders are charged and the impact they eventually will have on the timetable.

• The basic work description. This should be extremely detailed, including everything from installing phone jacks to the final cleaning of your

CREATE A RECORD

You have a team of highly qualified professionals building your home, but the ultimate responsibility is on your shoulders. So keep track of the project. Organize a binder to keep all of your samples, change orders and documents together. Make copies for yourself of all communication with your suppliers and contractor. Take notes from conversations and send them to the contractor. This can help eliminate confusion before a problem occurs.

TRUTH ABOUT CHANGE ORDERS

The building process demands an environment that allows for changes as plans move from paper to reality. Although you can control changes through careful planning in the preliminary stages of design and bidding, budget an extra seven to 10 percent of the cost of the home to cover change orders. Changes are made by talking to the contractor, not someone working at the site.

home. A comprehensive list of specified materials should be given, if it hasn't already been provided by your architect.

• Allowances. Are they realistic? This is one place where discrepancies will be evident. Is Contractor A estimating $75,000 for cabinets while Contractor B is stating $150,000?

• Warranty. A one-year warranty, effective the date you move in, is standard in this area.

THE TIMELINE

This changeable document will give you a good indication if and when things will go wrong.

Go to the site often enough to keep track of the progress according to the timeline. Do what you need to do to keep the project on schedule. One of the main causes of delays and problems is late decision-making by the homeowner. If you wait until three weeks prior to cabinet installation to order your cabinets, you can count on holding up the entire process by at least a month. (You'll also limit your options to cabinets that can be delivered quickly.)

BUILDING SUPPLIER: EARTH

Some of the most popular materials around today are those that have been here forever. While our homes may contain the modern technology and up-to-date amenities, natural materials, such as marble, granite, stone and rich woods, provide the backbone for these homes. Italian tile can bring you a piece of that Tuscan villa you dream about, granite surfaces or heavy wood cabinetry can bring a bit of nature into your otherwise sleek and modern kitchen, and the visible use of certain types of stone throughout your home can pay tribute to the architectural heritage of the area.

Keep in mind, though, that whatever materials you are using, different times of the year dictate different prices. The cost of lumber, for example, traditionally goes up in late spring to mid-summer. Good builders might also be able to predict when there will be occasional shortages in such products as drywall and brick, and plan accordingly. They will also know when to buy certain items in bulk to decrease your overall costs. Also ask your builder about new products, such as manufactured, or faux, stone, which yield many of the same benefits of its natural counterpart, but at a reduced cost.

CREATING A CUSTOM HOME

While every home project is different, here's one example of some of the costs involved in building a custom home. This one is for construction of a 10,000 sq. ft. home with brick and stone veneer and a slate roof.

• **Rough Lumber and Exterior Trim:** $110,000
• **Carpentry:** $100,000
• **Steel and Ornamental Iron:** $12,500
• **Windows:** Skylight, $1,500 Windows and doors, $75,000
• **Slate Roof:** $140,000
• **Radiant Heat:** $12,500
• **Security System:** $5,000
• **Masonry Veneer:** $215,000
• **Wood floors:** $30,000
• **Tile:** Ceramic tile, $30,000 Hearth and surround, $10,500
• **Cabinets and Vanities:** $125,000
• **Interior trim:** Mantel, $10,900 Wine rack, $3,000 Closets, $8,000

SOURCE FOR HISTORIC PROPERTIES

The National Trust for Historic Preservation
1785 Massachusetts Avenue, N.W.
Washington, DC 20036
202.588.6000

Having a home listed on the National Register doesn't restrict homeowners from demolishing or making changes (local restrictions do that), but offers possible financial assistance and tax credits for renovations, and limited protection against federal 'takings.' The organization sponsors programs, publishes newsletters and books, and advocates preservation.

THE TEAR-DOWN TREND

Land for new residential construction is getting harder to find, and "tear-down" renovations are becoming more common. There are often mixed emotions in an existing neighborhood as old structures come down. If you are considering a "tear-down" property, be sure you work with a builder and architect who are sensitive to the character of the neighborhood, and will help you build a home that fits in.

THE SECOND TIME'S A CHARM

Renovating a home offers the unique excitement of reinventing an old space to serve a new, enhanced purpose. It's an evolutionary process, charged with creative thinking and bold ideas. If you enjoy a stimulating environment of problem solving and decision making, and you're prepared to dedicate the needed time and resources, remodeling will result in a home which lives up to all of your expectations. You'll be living in the neighborhood you love, in a home that fits your needs.

A WORD ABOUT FINANCING OF REMODELING PROJECTS

Payment schedules in remodeling contracts typically require a deposit or a first payment at the start of the project, with subsequent payments due monthly or in conjunction with the progress of the work.

It is within your rights to withhold a negotiated percentage of the contract price until you're satisfied that the terms of the contract have been met and the work has been inspected. This should be stipulated in the written contract. Ten percent is the average amount to be held back, but is negotiated based on the overall size of the project.

Remodeling specialists who attract a quality-minded clientele are kept abreast of the most attractive remodeling loans on the market by lenders who specialize in these products. Ask your remodeler for referrals to these financial institutions.

RESTORE, RENEW

Many homeowners at the beginning of the new century are attracted to the historic architecture in older neighborhoods. Maturity and classicism are factors that persuade homeowners to make an investment in an old home and restore, renovate or preserve it, depending on what level of involvement interests them and the significance of the house. Renovations include additions and updating or replacing systems in the house. Restorations involve restoring the building to the specifications original to the house. Preservation efforts preserve what's there.

Like any remodeling project, it's an emotional and personal experience, only more so. Staying within the confines of a certain period or style is difficult and time consuming. That's why it's crucial to find an experienced architect and builder who share a reverence for tradition and craftsmanship. At your interview, determine if his or her portfolio shows competence in this specialty. It's vital to find a professional who understands historic projects and knows experienced and qualified contractors and/or subcontractors who will do the work for you. Ask if he or she knows experienced contractors who work in historic districts and have relationships with knowledgeable, experienced craftsmen. If you want exterior features, like period gardens or terraces, ask if they will be included in the overall plan. Make sure he or she has sources for you to find period furnishings, sconce shades or chimney pots.

There are many construction and design issues particular to old homes. The historic renovation and preservation experts featured in the following pages bring experience, creativity and responsibility to each project.

THESE OLD HOUSES

Before you fall in love with an old house, get a professional opinion. Find out how much is salvageable before you make the investment. Can the wood be restored? Have the casings been painted too many times? Is the plaster wavy and buckled? Can the house support ductwork for central air conditioning or additional light sources?

Notable remodelers are often contacted for their expert advice prior to a real estate purchase, and realtors maintain relationships with qualified remodelers for this purpose. They also keep remodelers informed of special properties suitable for custom renovations as they become available.

LEAVING HOME

Remodelers overwhelmingly agree their clients are happier if they move to a temporary residence during all, or the most intensive part, of the renovation. The sight of the roof and walls being torn out, the constant banging and buzzing of tools, and the invasion of privacy quickly take their toll on children and adults who are trying to carry on family life in a house full of dust. Homeowners who are well-rested from living in clean, well-lighted temporary quarters enjoy better relationships with each other, their remodeler and subcontractors.

Common hideaways are rental homes, suite-type hotels, the unoccupied home of a relative, or a long vacation trip. ■

HOME BUILDER SOURCES

Greater Houston Builders Association 9511 W. Sam Houston Pkwy. N. Houston, TX 77064 281.970.8970 281.970.8971 (fax) www.ghba.org

National Association of the Remodeling Industry (NARI) 847.298.9200 www.nari.org

CLEANUP TIME: Now or Later?

Your remodeling contract should be specific about cleanup. Will the site be cleaned up every day, or at the end of the project? Everyday cleanup may add to the price, but is well worth the extra expenditure.

STUCCO
KEYSTONE

STUCCO
QUIONS

36" HIGH
DECOR
W.I. RAIL

1820

1'-6"

2-3050

9322

PLAN WELL

BUILD WITH T

They say that purchasing a home is the most important decision one will make. Choosing the right builder for the job should be equally as important. Planning well and choosing a builder that understands your needs is a critical element for success. Tuscan Homes understands the need of today's homebuyer. Through artisanship and utilizing the latest cutting edge technology in building, we strive for perfection on every home we build.

Additonally, effective comminication is key during the building process. From start to completion we are there to insure not only

SCAN HOMES.

excellence in workmanship, but also an extraordinary experience. After all, you deserve it. It is your home we are building .

Tuscan Homes is a full service custom builder. Whether you need design assistance, lot finding, engineering, or just building on an existing lot, we can assist your needs. We also build spec homes in exclusive neighborhoods.

Call us for a free preliminary consultation. Live well, plan well. Choose Tuscan Homes as your premier custom builder. Together we can build your dream home!

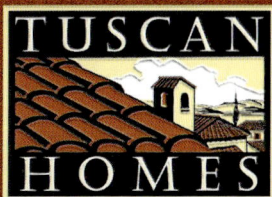

TUSCAN HOMES

713-647-9160

MICHAEL KELLY BUILDERS, INC.
CUSTOM HOMES

4010 Bluebonnet Blvd. Ste. 104 Houston, TX 77025
Tel. (713) 665-0250

OUR FRIEND.
OUR BUILDER.
for Life

PERFECT VISION

"Our vision of home may not be shared by everyone, but Stephen Hann definitely got it. Hann Builders brought our vision to life with their attention to detail, consummate professionalism and a sincere commitment to exceeding our expectations. The superb customer service we've experienced after closing has really cemented our on-going relationship. So now, from our new home, life has never looked better."

He'll be our "Builder For Life."
Dr. John & Rebecca Bergeron

HannBuilders

IRONWOOD HOMES

Nicholas A. Silvers

P.O. Box 22735
Houston, Texas
Ph: 713.871.8455
www.ironwoodhomes.com

THE 2002
HOME
BOOK
DESIGN
EXCELLENCE
AWARDS
GOLD
WINNER

"*... everything about my home

Custom
Home Builders

ALLEGRO BUILDERS..**(713) 880-8899**
1533 Heights Blvd., Houston   Fax:(713) 426-4686
See ad on page 112, 113
<u>Website:</u> www.allegrobuilders.com
<u>e-mail:</u> lambert@allegrobuilders.com

ALRAMCO CUSTOM HOMES & REMODELING ....**(281) 496-0496**
3715 Xenophone, Houston   Fax:(281) 496-2999
See ad on page 122, 123
<u>Website:</u> www.alramco.com
<u>e-mail:</u> luisramirez@alramco.com

B A S CONCEPTS LLP..**(713) 664-2600**
4545 Bissonnet, Suite 265, Bellaire   Fax:(713) 664-2601
See ad on page 124, 125
<u>Website:</u> www.basconcepts.com
<u>e-mail:</u> obatagower@basconcepts.com

GOSHY HOMES ....**(281) 364-0891**
30502 Thorsby Dr., Spring   Fax:(281) 419-9066
See ad on page 109
<u>Website:</u> www.goshyhomes.com
<u>e-mail:</u> goshyhomes@email.com

HAHNFELD-WITMER-DAVIS..**(713) 840-1001**
1717 St. James Place, Suite 200, Houston   Fax:(713) 840-7177
See ad on page 111
<u>Website:</u> www.hwdinc.com
<u>e-mail:</u> carolyn@hwdinc.com

HANN BUILDERS ....**(281) 980-0800**
12919 Southwest Freeway #110, Stafford   Fax:(281) 980-5630
See ad on page 103
<u>Website:</u> www.hannbuilt.com
<u>e-mail:</u> cherib@hannbuilt.com

IRONWOOD CUSTOM HOMES... ....**(713) 871-8455**
PO Box 22735, Houston   Fax:(713) 871-8538
See ad on page 104, 105
<u>Website:</u> www.ironwoodhomes.com

MCVAUGH CUSTOM HOMES, INC ....**(713) 682-2777**
6815 Northampton Way, Houston   Fax:(713) 682-1554
See ad on page 92D
<u>Website:</u> www.mcvaugh.com
<u>e-mail:</u> jim@mcvaugh.com

MEMORIAL BUILDERS ....**(713) 266-6500**
7670 Woodway, Ste. 344, Houston   Fax:(713) 266-7810
See ad on page 126, 127

MICHAEL KELLY BUILDERS INC ....**(713) 665-0250**
4010 Bluebonnet Blvd., Suite 104, Houston   Fax:(713) 665-0250
See ad on page 102
<u>Website:</u> www.michaelkellybuilders.com
<u>e-mail:</u> mjkelly32@netscape.net

PREMIER VICTORIAN HOMES, INC ....**(713) 862-7999**
323 W. 14th Street, Houston   Fax:(713) 862-3404
See ad on page 114
<u>Website:</u> www.premiervictorian.com
<u>e-mail:</u> premiervic@aol.com

ROHE & WRIGHT BUILDERS..**(713) 864-4040**
3000 Weslayan #111, Houston   Fax:(713) 864-4141
See ad on page 106, 107
<u>Website:</u> www.rohewright.com
<u>e-mail:</u> info@rohewright.com

continued on page **128**

GOSHY HOMES

Building Custom Homes in
Carlton Woods & Kingwood

·

30502 Thorsby Dr. Spring, TX 77386
281.364.0891

Photography by: Kelvin Lee

WATERMARK HOMES

❧

4545 Bissonnet Street
Bellaire, TX 77401
713.665.2263
www.watermarkbuilders.com

A L L E G R O

Homes by Allegro Builders combine

timeless design with

the finest in contemporary amenities.

Every Allegro home is built to

exacting specifications by

skilled craftsmen — you can see and feel

the quality everywhere you look.

CLIMATE
CONTROL

L ife in southern Texas can be challenging when you have to battle
Mother Nature. An unpredictable tornado season leads into the
hot, sticky days of summer, and somewhere in-between nature's friends,
with names like Charley and Francis, unload inches of rain and high winds
during tropical storm and hurricane season. For Houston home builders,
the challenge is during the construction process, insuring a safe home
that can endure the elements Mother Nature dishes out.

HomeB

Proper foundation construction and solid craftsmanship allows the home to withstand Houston's extreme weather conditions.

Photo courtesy of **Smith Custom Builders, Inc.**

uilding

A Foundation of Security

Moisture is a considerable factor for builders on the Gulf Coast. The "gumbo" soil is primarily clay based and is extremely sensitive to the area's fluctuation in moisture. During hurricane season, the soil expands, yet during the dry summer months, the soil contracts and cracks. Builders must take precautions during the foundation process of construction to insure the homes' security, often in the form of void boxes.

"These are four to five inch thick wax-coated cardboard spacers that are placed between the grid beams under the slab of the home," explained Doug Smith, president, Smith Custom Builders, Inc. "This is called the 'crush zone' because uplift from swelling caused by increased moisture content in the soil crushes the void boxes, but without lifting the slab off the grade beams and piers." Essentially, the tactic helps insure a home's foundation is safe from movement during the changing moisture levels.

Creating a moisture barrier before the foundation is poured is important as well. Smith applies a layer of plastic under the foundation before the concrete is laid. "Moisture in your foundation can force pressure through your flooring," explained Smith. Because coastal community homes rarely have basements, this pressure can ruin hardwood flooring. Over time, the hardwood, if glued directly to the concrete, cause the adhesive to no longer function, allowing the floor to buckle.

A warm Houston evening requires a feeling of comfort and serenity within the home.

Photo courtesy of **McVaugh Custom Homes, Inc.**

HomeB

Photo courtesy of **McVaugh Custom Homes, Inc.**

Because of the high moisture content and extreme temperatures in the Houston area, window selection is important. Aluminum windows will conduct heat and can cause an inconsistent indoor environment. Luis Ramirez, of Alramco Custom Homes & Remodeling suggests using vinyl or wood windows.

Seal of Approval

Heavy rains and high humidity levels also have builders taking extra precautions around windows and doors. With 90 percent of all home leaks originating in the area surrounding windows and doors, builders look to big name products to keep things dry. "We use Dupont's Tyvek® house-wrap and sticky tape to flash around the windows prior to their installation," said Jim McVaugh, president, McVaugh Custom Homes, Inc. Once the windows are installed they repeat the process again before the entire home is wrapped with Tyvek® and then again, the windows are wrapped and taped. "Our job is to insure moisture will remain outside of the home; it's a sign we've done our job well."

Rain will infiltrate any masonry material from stucco to brick to Hardiplank Siding,™ so when moisture does penetrate the outside material it needs somewhere to go. Layers of sheathing, along with the house wrap and tape all act as barriers to the moisture. "With the high moisture content in our air, we must use products that have high permeability. They must hold out bulk water, but allow moisture vapor to pass through," explained Doug Smith.

Pest Protection

The warm, moist Houston climate has also proved to be the perfect breeding ground for termites and cockroaches. Lambert Arceneaux, president, Allegro Builders, said pre-treating the foundation prior to construction and again around the perimeter of the home once construction is complete is essential to pest control. "We also use boric acid between the studs. It's an inexpensive way to keep cockroaches and termites out."

uilding

The Big Chill

No matter which builder you talk with, all agree that a high-tech HVAC system is an essential tool in surviving the fluctuating Houston climate. "It's important to select a system that will serve your home with efficiency and consistency, and sometimes that means spending a little more," said Luis Ramirez, partner, Alramco Custom Homes & Remodeling.

Selecting the proper system is just part of the process. The builder must determine where to place vents and air ducts for optimum results. "With the increase in vaulted ceilings and loft areas in today's luxury homes, it's important to consider the placement of air ducts," said Ramirez. Air vents are placed near or on the ceilings of homes with the idea that warm air

rises and cool air falls. Many builders suggest the incorporation of more vents in the home as well, to help with circulation concerns.

Ramirez feels the biggest challenge for builders in the Houston area is maintaining a consistent temperature throughout the home. Sometimes major decisions can be made to prevent energy efficiency problems before the opening stages of construction. "If a home faces north and south we do things during the planning stage to accommodate this factor," explained Ramirez. "But sometimes the homeowner is set on a certain view where the home must sit at the east-west angle. In this case we'll use thicker insulation on the west walls as well as better insulated windows." Combine those resources with a superior HVAC system and properly distributed and placed air vents, and a climate controlled, energy-efficient home will result. ■

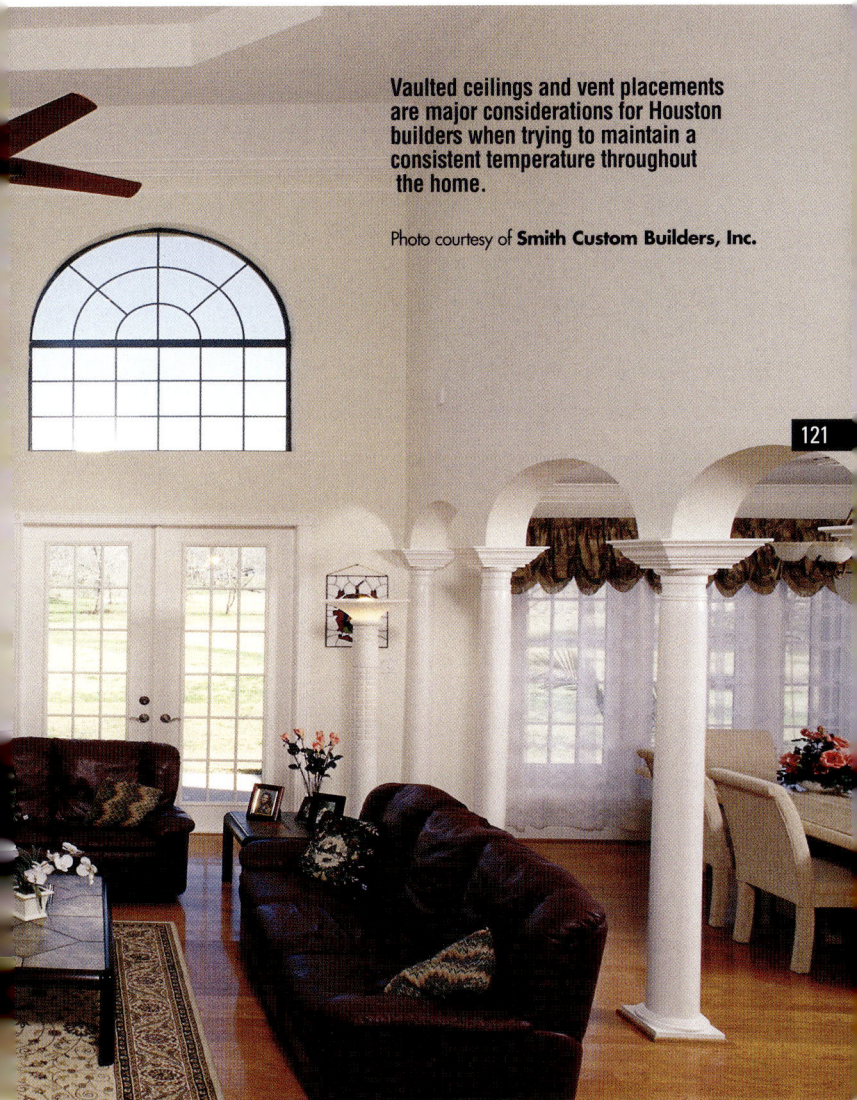

Vaulted ceilings and vent placements are major considerations for Houston builders when trying to maintain a consistent temperature throughout the home.

Photo courtesy of **Smith Custom Builders, Inc.**

uilding

- *New Construction*

- *Remodeling*

A Custom Home

A Carefully Orchestrated
Harmony Of Quality
Construction And Attention To Design

THE BEST HOMES ARE COLLABORATIVE EFFORTS. SINCE 1982 MEMORIAL BUILDERS HAS BEEN DOING JUST THAT. SIGNIFICANT HOMES HAVE BEEN CREATED IN THE MEMORIAL VILLAGES, TANGLEWOOD AND RIVER OAKS, MANY OF THEM IN CUL-DE-SAC ENCLAVES WE HAVE DEVELOPED.

MEMORIAL BUILDERS

for homes over one million dollars in value

Ask and we will find you antique French mantels, old doors from Mexico or carriage lamps from New Orleans. Memorial Builders' artisans can also reproduce classics or fabricate your own custom designs. Roofs are extra flashed and oversized superior grade copper water pipes are utilized. Extensive prewiring anticipates present and future electronics and telecommunications requirements. We are continually on site.

continued from page **108**

Custom
Home Builders

SMITH CUSTOM BUILDERS, INC ....**(713) 722-9600**
9320 Westview, Suite 1, Houston   Fax:(713) 722-8844
See ad on page 92B, 92C
Website: www.smithcustombuilders.com
e-mail: dsmith@smithcustombuilders.com

THOMPSON CUSTOM HOMES ....**(832) 327-0197**
11999 Katy Freeway, Ste. 420, Houston   Fax:(281) 558-3643
See ad on page 115
Website: www.thompsoncustomhomes.com
e-mail: bthompson@ev1.net

TUSCAN HOMES ....**(713) 647-9160**
1237 Blalock #103, Houston   Fax:(713) 784-3119
See ad on page 100,101
e-mail: jritchmond@ritchmondconstruction.com

WATERMARK HOMES ....**(713) 665-2263**
4545 Bissonnet St., Suite 115, Bellaire   Fax:(713) 665-2293
See ad on page 110
Website: www.watermarkbuilders.com

Remodeling
Specialists

BROTHERS STRONG, INC ....**(281) 469-6057**
12315 Ann Lane, Houston
See ad on page 130, 131
Website: www.brothersstrong.com
e-mail: deniset@brothersstrong.com

HOUSTON STRUCTURAL, INC ....**(713) 686-5900**
7632 Hammerly, Houston   Fax:(713) 686-5855
See ad on page 134, 135

REMODELING CONCEPTS, INC ....**(281) 499-9948**
1903 Maple Dale, Richmond   Fax:(281) 341-6277
See ad on page 129
Website: www.remodelingconcepts.biz
e-mail: info@remodelingconcepts.biz

WM. SHAW & ASSOC ....**(713) 666-1931**
4206 Law Street, Houston
See ad on page 132, 133
Website: www.wmshawandassoc.com
e-mail: wmshawandassoc@pdq.net

VISION.

Just one of the reasons we were named Houston Remodeler of the Year for 2003. But why not see for yourself? If you're ready to add on, build up or redo, give us a call. And see what a difference Strong vision can make.

2001
Chrysalis
Award

BROTHERS
STRONG

RESIDENTIAL
DESIGN ♦ BUILD

12315 ANN LANE
HOUSTON, TEXAS 77064
281.469.6057
WWW.BROTHERSSTRONG.COM

HOUSTON REMODELER OF THE YEAR

©2003

"A design build firm offering a solid partnership with experienced professionals whose skill and knowledge help you achieve your dreams for your home."

Full Service "Design/Build" remodeling specialists.
NARI National Contractor of the Year 2000
Member: NARI, NAHB, TAB, GHBA, & BBB

HOME BUILDING

Clapboard
Wood siding commonly used on the exterior of a home that overlaps horizontally.

Cornice
Any molded projection which crowns or finishes the part to which it is affixed, or an ornamental molding, usually of wood or plaster, running along the walls of a room just below the ceiling.

Continuous foundation
A foundation which supports a number of independent loads.

Double-hung window
A two-piece window that opens from the top or the bottom; the weight of each counterbalanced for ease of opening and closing.

Façade
The exterior of a home which is the architectural front, distinguished by an elaborate entryway or ornamental detail.

Gable
A vertical surface on the end of a building, usually adjoining a roof, which is triangular in shape.

Gable roof
A roof having a single slope on each side of a central ridge, with a gable at one or both ends.

Good morning stairs
In a full Cape house, the front stairs leading from the front hall to the attic rooms.

Lintel
A horizontal structure usually made of steel, stone or wood, over an opening which carries the weight of the wall above it. Generally found over doors, windows and fireplaces.

Load
A force, or system of forces, carried by a structure, or part of a structure.

Louver
A series of overlapping blades or slats that may be fixed or adjusted to admit light and/or air in varying degrees and to exclude rain or snow. Commonly found in shutters, windows and air vents.

Molding
A member of construction or decoration so treated as to introduce varieties of outline or contour in edges or surfaces. Also called mold.

Monkeytail
A vertical scroll at the bottom of a handrail of a stairway.

Mop-and-flop
A roofing technique in which the tiles or sheets used are initially placed upside down beside their final location, coated with adhesive, flipped over and applied to the substrate.

Mud Room
A small room adjacent to an exterior door, used for temporary storage of dirty or wet boots or outerwear.

Mullion
A vertical separation (often a support as well) of windows, doors or panels set in series.

Portico
A covered entrance whose roof is supported by columns. Also called a porticus or stoa.

Radiant Heating Systems
Systems for heating a room or space by means of heated surfaces such as floor panels heated by the flow of hot water or an electric current.

Trim
The visible woodwork of a room, such as the baseboards, skirting, cornices, casings, etc.

INTERIOR DESIGN

Mary A

"We worked with Mary Ann on two of our
Houston residences, a medical office and
a ranch house. Mary Ann is extremely skilled
in the planning phase of the project, and also is
an expert in materials and finishes. Her work
has a timeless quality that we continue to enjoy.
She helped realize our vision of beautifully
planned spaces with functional and well
designed furnishings."

Jackie and Sherwin Siff

"Mary Ann Bryan has designed two homes for us
and we have been very pleased. Her design skills
and her relationships with quality subcontractors,
craftspeople and design staff make it a pleasure
to work with her firm."

Dorothy and Gerald Smith

A Continuity

n Bryan
FASID

"Warm, yet elegant. Exquisite, yet comfortable
and very livable. Complete and beautiful.
These are but mere words which describe an
end product that we consider a perfect finish
to our new home by Mary Ann Bryan. Never
ending energy, constant smiles, desire to please
with design perfection. These likewise are just
words attempting to describe this incredible
lady and her firm."

Joe and Dianne Reeves

"We had strong ideas about what we wanted,
and Mary Ann understood immediately how to
translate our vision into reality. Trends in home
design come and go, but we think livable
elegance will never go out of style."

Punkin and Walter Hecht

Mary Ann Bryan
FASID

A Continuity of Elegance.

The Bryan Design Associates
5120 Woodway / Suite 8009
Houston, Texas 77056

Email: maryannb@bryandesigns.com
Tel. 713-513-2999
Fax. 713-961-5157

of Elegance.

Sherry Renfrow Moore's

Designer Showcase

TX Lic #5673

281.494.7469

Beauty is on the Inside

Transform a mundane room into a place of beauty. Fill in a newly constructed home's spaces with intelligent design and appropriate furnishings. Renovate historically significant rooms to make them livable for today's lifestyles. Interior designers perform all of these tasks and more, bringing your personality to life in the interior of your home.

These professionals will listen to your dreams and those of your family. They can bring the resources together to create rooms with special themes, such as a child's bedroom decorated as a favorite fairy tale, complete with rainbows painted on walls and clouds adorning the ceiling. Interior designers can convert under-utilized basements into wine tasting and storage areas that resemble a Tuscan café or a bistro in Provence. Envision what you want your room to be; your interior designer will make it happen.

Photo courtesy of **Designer Showcase**

WHERE STRUCTURE MEETS INSPIRATION

A great interior designer, like a great architect or builder, sees space creatively, applying years of education and experience to deliver a distinguished residence at the highest level of quality in an organized, professional manner. Intensely visual, these talented individuals imprint a home with the spirit and personality of the family living there.

A top quality interior designer who is licensed by the state is educated in the field of interior design, usually holding a bachelor's or master's degree in the subject. In addition to creating interiors, your interior designer also handles the "nuts and bolts" business end of the project. With skill and experience in placing and tracking orders, scheduling shipping, delivery and installation, the designer can bring your project to its perfect conclusion.

AN INTERIOR DESIGNER IS A TEAM MEMBER

Choose an interior designer when you select your architect, builder, and landscape architect. A skilled designer can collaborate with the architect on matters such as window and door location, appropriate room size, and practical and accent lighting plans. In new construction and remodeling, try to make your floor plan and furniture choices simultaneously, to avoid common design problems, such as traffic corridors running through a formal space or awkward locations of electrical outlets.

CREATE THE BEST CLIENT-DESIGNER RELATIONSHIP

Talk to the best interior designers in the area and they'll tell you how exciting and gratifying it is for them when a client is involved in the process. This is happening as more homeowners turn their attention to hearth and home, dedicating their tme and resources to achieve a style they love.

Define your needs, in terms of service and the end result. Have an interior designer involved during the architectural drawing phase of a new or renovation project, and get the process started early. Be clear about how much help you want from a designer. Some homeowners have a strong sense of what they want and simply need a consultant-type relationship. Others want significant guidance from a professional who will oversee the entire process.

Set up a relationship that encourages an open exchange of ideas. In pursuit of personal style, you need to trust a professional designer to interpret your

---

FIVE THINGS YOU SHOULD KNOW

1. Know what level of guidance you want: a person to handle every detail, someone to collaborate with you or simply an occasional consultation.
2. Know what you're trying to achieve. Start an Idea Notebook, filling it with pictures of rooms you like and don't like. This will help you define your style and stay true to your goal.
3. Know your budget. Prices of high-end furnishings know no upper limit. Adopt a "master plan" to phase in design elements if your tastes are outpacing your pocketbook.
4. Know what's going on. Always ask; don't assume. Design is not a mystical process.
5. Know yourself. Don't get blinded by beauty. Stay focused on what makes you feel "at home," and you'll be successful.

thoughts and needs. You must be comfortable saying, "No, I don't like that," and receptive to hearing, "I don't think that's a good idea."

Be forthcoming about your budget. Not all interiors are guided by a budget, but the majority are. Your designer must know and respect your financial parameters and priorities. If a gorgeous dining room table is a top priority, objets d' art can be added later as you find them. Prices of exquisite furniture, custom-carved cabinets, and other high-end furnishings know no upper limit. Be realistic about what you will spend and what you expect to achieve. Do some research in furniture stores and specialty shops, starting with those showcased in this book.

Be inquisitive as the design unfolds. This is a creative effort on your behalf, so let yourself enjoy it, understand it and be stimulated by it.

START THINKING VISUALLY: STOP, LOOK AND CLIP

Before you start scheduling initial interviews with interior designers, start compiling an Idea Notebook – it's the best tool for developing an awareness of your personal style. Spend a weekend or two with a pair of scissors, a notebook, and a stack of magazines, (or add a section to the Idea Notebook you made to inspire your architecture and building plans). Make this a record of your personal style. Include pictures of your favorite rooms, noting colors, fabrics, tile, carpet, fixtures, the way light filters through a curtain, anything that strikes your fancy. On those pictures, circle the design elements that you'd like to incorporate into your own home décor and make comments regarding those elements you don't care for. Think hard about what you love and loathe in your current residence. Start to look at the entire environment as a rich source of design ideas. Movies, billboards, architecture, clothing – all are fascinating sources for visual stimulation.

Then, when you hold that initial meeting, you, too, will have a book of ideas to share. Although a smart designer will be able to coax this information from you, it's tremendously more reliable to have visual representations than to depend on a verbal description. It also saves a tremendous amount of time.

THE INTERIOR DESIGN PROCESS: GETTING TO KNOW YOU

Give yourself time to interview at least two interior designers. Invite them to your home for a tour of your current residence and a look at items you wish to use in the new environment. If you're

TIME TO REDESIGN

The example below gives a general estimate of the costs involved in redesigning a 15 x 22 sq. ft. living room in a mid-scale price range.

Initial consultation: $500
Cost per hour (5 hour minimum): $100/hr
New rug (oriental or custom): $8,000
Furniture: Transitional (contemporary upholstery, traditional wood pieces)
Sofa, $3,000
Chairs (2), $1,000 ea.
Coffee table, $2,000
End tables (2), $1,000 ea.
Sofa table, $2,000
French Be'rgre chair, $3,000
Lamps (1 bronze, 2 porcelain): $1,200
Lighted wall sconces: $1,000
Artwork: $2,000
New paint (labor and paint): $1,500
Accessories: $3,000

Total: $31,700

139

Interior Design

building or remodeling, an interior designer can be helpful with your overall plans when he or she is given the opportunity to get involved early in the building process.

During the initial meeting, count on your intuition to guide you toward the best designer for you. Decorating a home is an intimate and very personal experience, so a comfortable relationship with a high degree of trust is absolutely necessary for a good result. You may adore what a designer did for a friend, but if you can't easily express your ideas, or if you feel he or she isn't interested in your point of view, don't pursue the relationship. Unless you can imagine yourself working with a designer two or three homes from now, keep interviewing.

You may wish to hire a designer for one room before making a commitment to do the whole house.

Some designers maintain a high degree of confidentiality regarding their clients, but if possible, get references and contact them, especially clients with whom they've worked on more than one home. Be sure to ask about the quality of follow-up service.

Be prepared to talk in specific terms about your project, and to honestly assess your lifestyle. For a home or a room to work well, function must be considered along with the evolving style. Designers ask many questions; some of them may be:

• What function should each room serve? Will a living room double as a study? Will a guest room also be an exercise area?

• What kind of relationship do you want to establish between the interior and the landscape?

• Style: Formal, casual or a bit of both?

• Are you comfortable with color?

• Are you naturally organized or disorganized?

• What kind of art do you like? Do you own art that needs to be highlighted or displayed in a certain way? Do you need space for a growing collection?

• Do you feel at home in a dog-eared, low maintenance family room or do you soothe your soul in an opulent leather chair, surrounded by rich cabinetry and Oriental rugs?

• What kind of furniture do you like? Queen Anne, Contemporary, American Arts and Crafts, casual wicker, or eclectic mixing of styles?

• What words describe the feeling you want to achieve? Cheerful, cozy, tranquil, elegant, classic?

PROFESSIONAL DESIGNATIONS

ASID (American Society of Interior Designers
Texas Gulf Coast Chapter
Chapter Office:
Sarah Eilers
5120 Woodway,
Suite 122
Houston, TX
77056-1708
Phone:
713.626.1470
Fax: 713.965.0846
asidtgcc@
mindspring.com

IIDA (International Interior Design Association)
International Headquarters
998 Merchandise Mart
Chicago, IL 60654
312.467.1950
www.iida.org
email:
IIDAhq@iida.org
Offers referrals to area homeowners.

Designers who add ASID or IIDA after their names are certified members of the organization.

COMPUTING THE INTERIOR DESIGN FEE

Designers use individual contracts, standard contracts drawn up by the American Society of Interior Designers (ASID), or letters of agreements as legal documents. The ASID contract outlines seven project phases – programming, schematic, design development, contract documents, contract administration, project representation beyond basic services, and additional services. It outlines the designer's special responsibilities, the owner's responsibilities, the fees agreed upon, and the method of payments to the designer, including reimbursement of expenses.

Payment deadlines vary. Payments may be due at the completion of each project phase, on a monthly or quarterly basis, or as orders are made. You can usually expect to pay a retainer or a 50 percent deposit on goods as they are ordered, 40 percent upon the start of installation, and the balance when the job is completed.

Design fees, which may be based on "current market rate," are also computed in various ways. They may be charged on a flat fee or hourly basis, or may be tied to retail costs. Expect fees of approximately $100 an hour, varying by experience, reputation and workload. A designer's fee may also be commission-based, which is when a percentage of the cost of the project is added to compensate the designer. When charging by the fixed or hourly fee methods, designers may also add commission to items they purchase for the project. A designer's fees may also be based on the square footage of the area to be designed or decorated. Make sure you understand your fee structure early on.

If you work with a designer at a retail store, a design service fee ranging from $100 to $500 may be charged and applied against purchases.

FROM THE MIND'S EYE TO REALITY

Once you've found a designer who you like and trust, and have signed a clear, specific agreement, you're ready to embark on the adventure.

A good designer knows his or her way around the masses of products and possibilities. Such a person will guide you through upscale retail outlets and to craftspeople known only to a fortunate few in the trade. You can be a "kid in a candy store."

Just as you've allowed time to carefully consider and reconsider architectural blueprints, temper your enthusiasm to rush into decisions regarding your interiors. Leave fabric swatches where you see them day after day. Look at paint samples in daylight,

ASID CERTIFICATION

Currently, 22 states and two jurisdictions have laws regulating the practice of interior design and/or the use of a title.

They are:

ALABAMA
ARKANSAS
CALIFORNIA
COLORADO
CONNECTICUT
FLORIDA
GEORGIA
ILLINOIS
KENTUCKY
LOUISIANA
MAINE
MARYLAND
MINNESOTA
MISSOURI
NEVADA
NEW JERSEY
NEW MEXICO
NEW YORK
PUERTO RICO
TENNESSEE
TEXAS
VIRGINIA
WASHINGTON, DC
WISCONSIN

DESIGNER OR DECORATOR?

We hear the terms "interior designer" and "interior decorator" frequently, but the two are not interchangeable. The difference between them lies in the amount of training each has and what they are allowed to do. An interior designer is a professionally trained space planner, often going through a two-year long apprenticeship and a lengthy exam before they can practice as an interior designer on their own.

An interior decorator, on the other hand, can only work with surface decoration – paint, fabric, furnishings, lighting and other materials. Because no license is required, upholsterers, housepainters, and other tradespeople also claim the name "decorator."

EMBRACE THE MASTER PLAN

Gone are the days when area homeowners felt the need to move into a "finished" interior. They take their time now, letting the flow of their evolving lifestyle and needs guide them along the way.

evening light and artificial light. If possible, have everyone in the family "test sit" a kitchen chair for a week before ordering the whole set, and play with furniture placement. This small investment of time will pay handsomely in the end.

Be prepared to wait for your interiors to be installed. It's realistic to allow eight months to complete a room, and eight to 12 months to decorate an entire home.

Decide if you want your interiors to be installed piecemeal or all at once. Many designers recommend waiting for one installation, if you have the patience. Homeowners tend to rethink their original decisions when pieces are brought in as they arrive. By waiting for one installation, they treat themselves to a stunning visual and emotional thrill. ■

DIANA S. WALKER

INTERIOR DESIGN

Diana S. Walker, ASID
3815 Garrott, #12 • Houston, TX 77006
713/520-1775 • 713/520-1197 FAX • dwalkerdesign@aol.com

Interior
Designers

THE BRYAN DESIGN ASSOCIATES...**(713) 513-2999**
5120 Woodway, Suite 8009, Houston   Fax:(713) 963-5157
See ad on page 136B, 136C, 146
<u>e-mail:</u> maryannb@bryandesigns.com

ELIMA DESIGNS..**(713) 529-8899**
2480 Times Blvd., Ste. 210, Houston   Fax:(713) 529-3004
See ad on page 145
<u>e-mail:</u> saima@elimadesign.com

ILLUMINATIONS LIGHTING DESIGN ....**(713) 863-1133**
607 Durham Drive, Houston   Fax:(713) 863-0044
See ad on page 147, 179
<u>Website:</u> www.illuminationslighting.com
<u>e-mail:</u> tom@illuminationslighting.com

MILLER DESIGN ....**(713) 667-0700**
4809 Beech, Bellaire   Fax:(713) 661-7993
See ad on page 152
<u>e-mail:</u> mil81686@aol.com

SHERRY RENFROW MOORE'S DESIGNER SHOWCASE ....**(281) 494-7469**
12705 S. Kirkwood, Ste. 211, Stafford   Fax:(281) 242-2628
See ad on page 136D, 255, C3
<u>Website:</u> www.designershowcasewow.com
<u>e-mail:</u> general@designershowcasewow.com

DIANA S. WALKER INTERIOR DESIGN ....**(713) 520-1775**
3815 Garrott #12, Houston   Fax:(713) 520-1197
See ad on page 143
<u>e-mail:</u> dwalkerdesign@aol.com

Elima Designs

Interior Design Services

Elima Designs

Residential & Commercial Design

2480 Times Blvd. Suite 210 Houston, TX 77005
Phone 713-529-8899   Fax 713-529-3004
saima@elimadesign.com

148

DESIGNER SHOWCASE

Sherry Renfrow Moore:
"In keeping with the grand elegance of this custom home, two-story Corinthian columns were designed in the entry, creating a unique sculptural statement. Handcarved Texas limestone was chosen for its density and color. Traditionally made in segments, each column was carved in a single piece. Honed, crosscut travertine interspersed with black granite creates a spacious flow throughout the ground floor. We also custom designed and faux painted the wrought iron that winds from the gracious staircase on the left throughout the second story."

Interior

Photo by **Bruce Glass**

Design

THE BRYAN
DESIGN ASSOCIATES

Mary Ann Bryan:

"In this newly purchased home, our clients were presented with a master bedroom that contained a claustrophobic alcove for their bed. Our solution was to have a window installed (the room was on the second floor, with electric wiring directly in sight of the window). We designed a special frosted glass piece that concealed the wires, but that left a portion of clear glass so they could see the wonderful magnolia tree that was outside. We lit the room with wall lamps allowing the full use of the tops of small nightstands, created a soft headboard and then completed the furnishings."

Interio

ELIMA DESIGNS

Saima Seyar:

"The client's daughter was particularly attached to a mural scene airbrushed at a local restaurant frequented by her family. To stay within the client's budget, the challenge was to create the mural by hand painting and to make it seem as if it was a combination of airbrush and watercolor. The girl was in an age transition period. She was concerned about having a room that was appropriately feminine and fun, but also wanting to maintain a look that would last through her teenage years. The inset in the ceiling was utilized to create a fun environment in her bedroom. The project demanded placement detail, using one of the light bulbs as the sun's image. Since the ceiling fan was in the center of the inset, the garden was created around the fan."

Design

New Fresh Classic

Built-in Character

R · H · O · N · D · A

MILLER

D · E · S · I · G · N

7 1 3 · 6 6 7 · 0 7 0 0

Bellaire Bungalo Transformec

The Ashley Group Luxury Home Resource Collection

The Ashley Group (www.theashleygroup.com) is pleased to offer as your final destination when searching for home improvement and luxury resources the following **Home Books** in your local market. Available now: *Seattle, Boston, San Francisco Bay Area, Orange County, Kansas City, Connecticut/Westchester County and Houston among others.* These comprehensive, hands-on guides to building, remodeling, decorating, furnishing, and landscaping a luxury home, are required reading for the serious and selective homeowner. With more than 400 full-color, beautiful pages, the **Home Book** series in each market covers all aspects of the building and remodeling process, including listings of hundreds of local industry professionals, accompanied by informative and valuable editorial discussing the most recent trends.

Order your copies today and make your dream come true!

INTERIOR DESIGN

Art Deco
A popular design style during the 1920s and 1930s characterized by simple geometric patterns.

Chinoiserie
With a Chinese influence.

Faux finishing
(pronounced 'foe'- meaning fake), is the art of deceiving the onlooker to think he or she is seeing something that is not really there, similar to trompe l'oleil, but it is a simpler form of imitation as opposed to a large scale optical illusion. Its purpose is to simulate real raw materials such as wood, stone and marble using different paints, textures, colors and techniques.

Feng Shui
A traditional Chinese technique for planning the layout of a building and designing rooms within it so as to be in harmony with nature and its surroundings.

Italian Murano glass
High-quality silicate sand used to make the glass is imported from France and Switzerland. It is mixed with sodium carbonate and calcium and borax from the United States. Sodium nitrate and antimony are used to obtain clear glass and diverse mineral oxides are mixed together in order to obtain the hundreds of different shades and colors we see today.

Trompe l'Oleil
(pronounced - trump loy) A French term, which translates to "mislead the eye." In design, trompe l'oeil murals are paintings, usually on a wall, ceiling or floor, that when viewed from the right place, should deceive the viewer into thinking they are seeing something three-dimensional.

Venetian plaster
Italian, or Venetian, plaster is a natural mineral wall finish composed of marble dust, slaked lime and water. It can be processed to achieve different looks from a matte finish to a high polish, similar to marble.

Juxtapose
To place side-by-side or together in a space.

Turnkey
A job in which all the work, decorating and furnishing of the home is complete so that it is ready for immediate habitation.

Queen Anne style
Part of the early colonial style of decorating, the walls are usually painted in light colors, paneled or wallpapered. Large, bold classical patterns such as medallions, ornamental discs and ovals, fans, floral swags and pineapples are used in the wallpaper as well as other wall treatments. The appropriate fabrics for upholstery are tapestry, velvet, brocade, extensive needlework and leather. Drapery fabrics include crewel embroidery, hand-blocked linen, silk and worsted damask, velvet, and brocade. Popular period colors for both upholstery and draperies are full-bodied burgundy, green, and yellow.

Window treatments
Any number of decorative elements added to windows: draperies, valences, finials, shutters, blinds, etc.

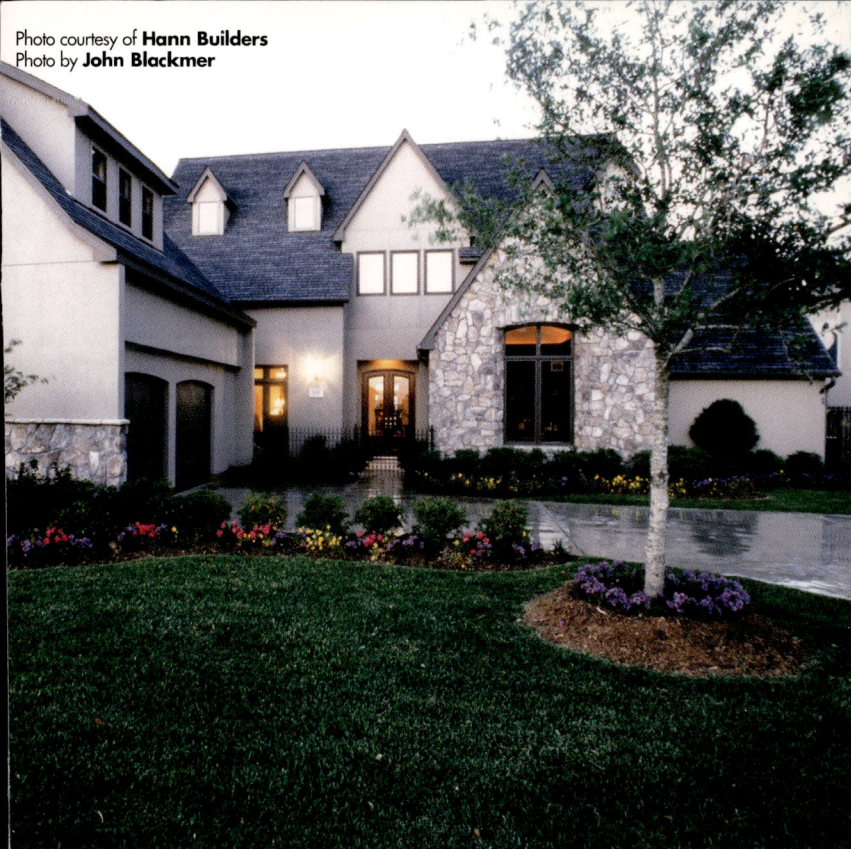

LANDSCAPING

Exterior Worlds

L A N D S C A P E

THE GARDEN SPEAKS VOLUMES WITHOUT
UTTERING A WORD.

Whether you prefer a touch of whimsy or traditional designs,
Exterior Worlds can create, develop and maintain your ideal garden.

EXTERIOR WORLDS
LANDSCAPE

phone 713.827.2255

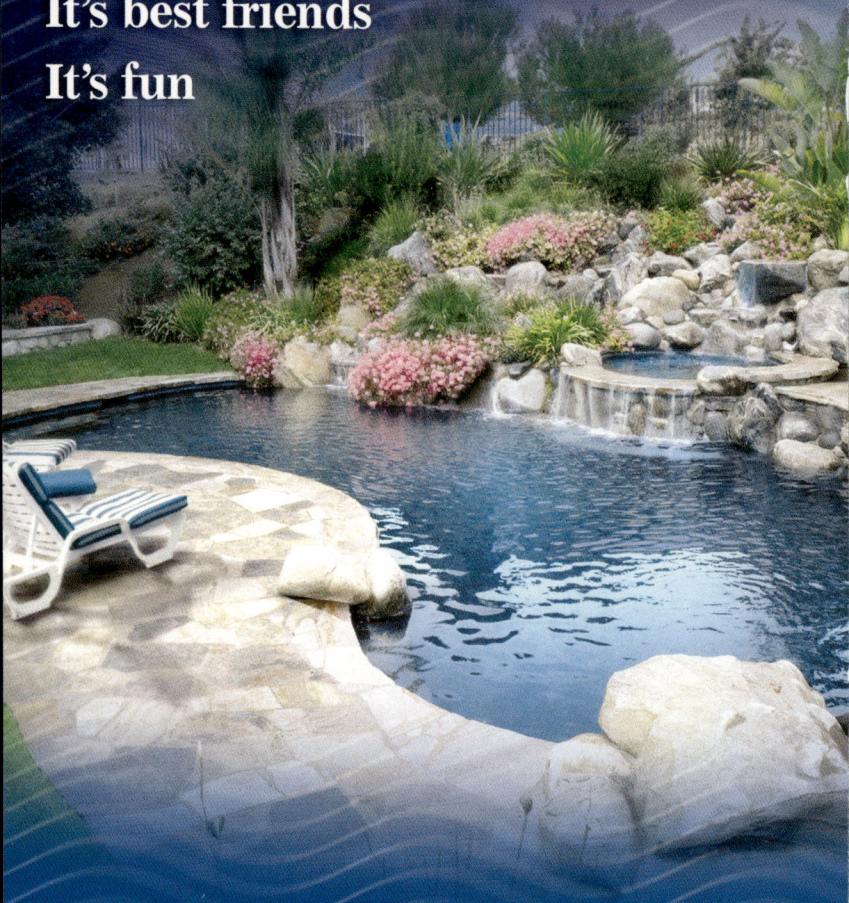

It's natural beauty
It's pure pleasure
It's best friends
It's fun

ANTHONY & SYLVAN POOLS
It's Where America Swims™

877-SAY-SWIM
www.anthonysylvan.com

Visit one of our 6 showrooms

houston • kingwood • katy/cinco ranch • clearlake
missouri city/sugar land • the woodlands

Est. 1946 | NASDAQ: SWIM | 350,000 pools built nationwide
Computerized design | 100% financing available

Nature's Way

You can control which site you buy, but you really can't control the site itself. Landscape is a living thing – transforming with the seasons, evolving or decaying over time, in tune with a home or fighting to destroy it. The ultimate goal is to build a home that complements the environment, and works with it rather than against it. Landscape architects and contractors are trained professionals who will work with your architect and builder to create the setting that you envision.

It's important to find a landscape architect and contractor who know the lay of the land, the peculiarities of your particular climate and the needs of your ecosystem. Whether you're taking advantage of spectacular views or creating them yourself through wondrous gardens and pools, walkways and driveways, your landscaping professional will bring in the trees, plants and stone to turn your plot of land into spectacular natural surroundings.

Landscaping

THE VISION

First you choose your views, then you build your home. To create a harmonious balance between your home and its surroundings, your architect should be invited to visit the site of your new home, and to meet with your landscape architect. The site can often serve as a catalyst, inspiring a design that responds to the uniqueness of the site. When all the team members are included, important details can be discussed and settled, leading to best results for you and your family.

A PARTY OF GARDENS

As gardening attracts more devotees, people are rediscovering the satisfaction of creating imaginative gardens. Some ideas: butterfly gardens, fragrance gardens, moonlight gardens and Japanese gardens.

GETTING BACK TO THE GARDEN

Think of the land as a canvas for a work of environmental art. Think of the landscape professional as an artist who uses nature to translate your needs and desires into a living, breathing reality. A formal English garden or seemingly artless arrangements of native plantings, a winding cobblestone walkway leading from a hand-laid brick driveway – these are the kinds of possibilities you can explore. When you work with a professional who is personally committed to superior work and service, designing a landscape is full of creativity, new ideas and satisfying results.

GETTING A LANDSCAPE STARTED

Selecting a landscape professional to create and maintain a distinctive landscape is one of the most important decisions you'll make as a homeowner. In making your decision, consider these questions:

• Do you want to hire a landscape architect or a landscape designer? Landscape architects have met the criteria to be registered by the state. Many hold university degrees in landscape architecture. A landscape designer generally has had training and/or experience in horticulture and landscaping and may also have a background in art.

• Do you want full service? If you want to work with one source, from design to installation to maintenance, only consider those who offer comprehensive service.

Allow approximately one month to interview at least two professionals before making a decision. Start even earlier if you plan to install a swimming pool, which should be dug the same time as the foundation of a new home.

Invite the professional to your home to acquaint him or her with your tastes and personality. Be prepared to answer questions like:

• Do you prefer a formal or informal feel? The formality of symmetrical plantings or the informal look of a natural area?

• Is there a place or feeling you'd like to recreate? Summers spent at the cottage? Your childhood home?

• What colors do you like? Your answer may impact the flowers chosen for your gardens.

• Are you a gardener? Would you like to be? If you're fond of flower, herb or vegetable gardening, your landscape professional will plan and build the appropriate garden.

• How will you use the space? Will children use the backyard for recreation? Will you entertain outdoors? If so, will it be during the day or at night? Do you envision a pool, spa, gazebo or tennis courts there?

• Are you fond of lawn statuary, fountains or other ornamental embellishments?

• What architectural features must be considered? A wrap-around porch, large picture windows? Brick or stone exteriors?

• To what extent will you be involved in the process? Most landscape architects and designers are happy to encourage your involvement in this labor of love. There is a great deal of pleasure to be derived from expressing your personality through the land. A lifelong hobby can take root from this experience. Landscapers say their clients often join garden clubs after the completion of their project, and that many of their rehabbing jobs are done for clients who are already avid gardeners.

Landscape professionals expect that you will want to see a portfolio and inquire about their styles and experience. You may wish to request permission to visit sites of their installed landscapes. If you have special concerns, such as environmental issues, ask if the landscape professional has any experience in such areas.

COMPUTING LANDSCAPE FEES

It's easy to be caught off guard when you get a landscape proposal – it is a significant investment. Therefore, be sure you create a workable budget with your landscape professional before the project begins.

To give the outside of your home the appropriate priority status, plan to invest 10 to 25 percent of the cost of a new home and property in the landscaping. Although landscape elements can be phased in year after year, expect that the majority of the cost will be incurred in the first year. Maintenance costs must also be considered.

Billing practices vary among professionals and depend on the extent of the services you desire. Some charge a one-time fee for a contract that includes everything, some charge a flat design fee up front, others charge a design fee which is waived if you select them to complete the project, and still others build a design fee into the installation and/or maintenance cost.

THE PRICE OF BEING GREEN

What might it cost to create a new paver patio and walk, retaining wall and 600 sq. ft. of new planting beds along the front foundation?
Design contract fees - $500
Cut Lanonstone retaining wall (85 face sq. ft.) - $4,130
Concrete paver patio and walkway (480 sq. ft.) - $7,785
Planting development (600 sq. ft.) - $9,000
Includes shrubs, four mid-size trees, perennials, annual beds and sod.
Landscape management of one-half acre site for one season - $3,648
Weekly mowing, trimming and disposal; monthly pavement edging; monthly cultivation of open beds; preventative weed control; granular fertilization of beds; pruning; weekly dead heading of faded flowers, groundcover maintenance, turf fertilization.

Total - $25,063

157

A PROFESSIONAL DEVELOPS AN ENVIRONMENT

While you're busy imagining glorious gardens, your landscaper will be assessing practical issues like grading and drainage, the location of sewers, utility lines and existing trees, where and when the sun hits the land and the quality of the soil.

This important first step, the site analysis, should take place before construction has even begun, in the case of a new house. Site work helps ensure that the blueprints for your house won't make your landscape dreams impossible to achieve, and vice versa. If you've told your builder you want a breakfast nook, you'll probably get one regardless of the fact that it requires taking out a tree you value.

If you're considering installing a custom driveway or sidewalk, this early stage is the time to inform your builder. Ask your builder not to do construction outside the building envelope. You and your landscape professionals should design and build your driveway and walkways.

Expect the design process to take at least six weeks. During this time, the designer is developing a plan for the hardscape, which includes all of the man-made elements of your outdoor environment, and the many layers of softscape, which are the actual plantings. You can expect to be presented with a plan view that is workable and in harmony with your home, as well as your budget.

Hardscape elements, like irrigation systems and pavements, will be installed first, before a new house is completely finished. Softscape will go in later.

At the end of the first phase of your project, do not be surprised if the land does not look "complete." A landscape should be given time in the hands of nature to mature: three years for perennials, five years for shrubs and 15 years for trees.

LUXURY LIVING WITH A CUSTOM-DESIGNED POOL

The beauty and value of a custom-designed swimming pool are unmatched. A welcome design element to the landscape, a pool adds to the overall property value of the residence and creates greater use and enjoyment of the yard. As area families spend more of their leisure time at home, a pool answers their dreams of living well at home.

Deciding to build a swimming pool is best done as a new home is being designed so the pool can enhance the home and landscape architecture. By integrating the pool into the overall scheme, you'll be able to establish a realistic budget. One of the biggest mistakes homeowners make when purchasing

LIGHTING YOUR LOT

"Less is more" is the best philosophy when designing an outdoor lighting system. Today's beautiful, functional fixtures are themselves worthy of admiration, but their purpose is to highlight the beauty of your home while providing safe access to your property. Well-established lighting companies and specialty companies offer extensive landscape lighting product lines.

THE FINAL EVALUATION

When the landscape is installed, conduct a final, on-site evaluation. You should evaluate the finished design, find out what elements will be installed later and learn more about how the plan will evolve over time. You, the landscape designer or architect, project manager, and maintenance manager should be involved.

a pool is not initially getting all the features they want. It's difficult and costly to add features later.

The design process is time consuming. You may have four or more meetings with your pool professional before finalizing the design. Pool projects can be started at almost any time of year, so avoid getting caught in the busy season, spring to summer. Start getting approvals in January if you want to be enjoying your pool in the summer. The building process takes about two months, after obtaining permits. You should plan to have your pool dug at the same time as the home foundation. Pools are often accompanied by surrounding decks, so make sure your landscape architect, pool builder and hardscape contractor are coordinating efforts to construct both.

OUTDOOR LIVING

Today's homeowners, having invested the time and resources to create a spectacular environment, are ready to "have it all" in their own backyards.

Popular features of today's upscale homes include outdoor living rooms, screened rooms, gazebos and custom-made jungle gyms that will grow with your children. The extended living space perfectly suits our "cocooning" lifestyle, offering more alternatives for entertaining, relaxation and family time at home. Many new homes tout outdoor living space as a most tantalizing feature.

Multi-level terraces and decks offer extra living space and are functional enough to host almost any occasion. With thoughtful and proper design, they fulfill our dreams of an outdoor getaway spot. A multi-level deck built up and around mature trees can feel like a tree house. A spa built into a cedar deck, hidden under a trellis, can give you the feel of being in a far-off paradise.

Landscaping features that will compliment your outdoor living space include Koi ponds and imaginative theme gardens, such as moonlight, Zen, butterfly, fragrance, two-color and native plant gardens.

With so many options available, outdoor living provides a unique opportunity for homeowners to give their creativity free. However, consult with your landscape architect and contractor before deciding on these outdoor features. Some outdoor living space and garden options will function better than others, depending on what area of the country you reside in.

THINKING ABOUT OUTDOOR LIVING

If you're interested in pursuing any of the ideas mentioned above, then the first step is to arrange an on-site meeting with a landscape architect or a

EVERY KID'S FANTASY

In a yard with plenty of flat area: A wood construction expandable play system with: several slides, bridges to connect structures, a tic-tac-toe play panel, three to four swings, climbing ropes, fire pole, gymnastics equipment (trapeze, turning bar), sandbox pit, and a built-in picnic table with benches. Price Tag: around $26,000

In a smaller yard: a wood construction expandable play system with: a small fort, three swings, climbing ropes and two slides. Price Tag: around $6,500

GARDENER'S EDENS

Visit this garden for ideas and inspiration.

Houston Arboretum and Nature Center 4501 Woodway Dr. Houston, TX 77024-7708 713.681.8433

A TYPICAL LANDSCAPE DESIGN TIMETABLE

- **One to two weeks to get the project on the boards**

+

- **One to two weeks to do the actual site and design work and prepare plans**

+

- **One week to coordinate calendars and schedule presentation meeting**

+

- **One to two weeks to leave the plans with the client and get their feedback**

+

- **One week to incorporate changes, create and get approval on a final design**

=

FIVE TO EIGHT WEEKS

WHY YOU NEED AN ARBORIST

It's not just your kids, dogs and the neighborhood squirrels trampling through your yard during construction. Excavation equipment, heavy trucks and work crews can spell disaster for your trees. Call an arborist before any equipment is scheduled to arrive and let him develop a plan that will protect the trees, or remove them if necessary.

licensed contractor who is an expert in landscape building. An experienced professional will guide you through the conceptualization by asking questions like these:

- Why are you building the structure or specialty garden? For business entertaining, family gatherings, child or teen parties, private time?

- Do you envision a secluded covered area, a wide open expanse or both?

- Do you want a single level or two or more levels (the best option for simultaneous activities)?

- Will it tie in with current or future plans?

- How do you want to landscape the perimeter?

- Do you want a chiminea to be included in your outdoor living room, a certain variety of sand for your Zen garden or specific wood used in creating your gazebo?

Don't let obstacles block your thinking. Your gas grill can be moved. Decks are often built around trees and can convert steep slopes into usable space.

Once a design has been settled upon, expect at least three to four weeks to pass before a gazebo or other living space is completed. In the busy spring and summer months, it most likely will take longer. The time required to get a building permit (usually two to four weeks) must also be considered.

If you're landscaping during this time, be sure to coordinate the two projects well in advance. Building can wreck havoc on new plantings and your lawn will be stressed during construction.

DISTINCTIVE OUTDOOR SURFACES

Driveways, walkways, patios and hardscape features were once relegated to "last minute" status, with a budget to match. Today they are being given the full and careful attention they deserve. A brick paver driveway can be made to blend beautifully with the color of the brick used on the house. Natural brick stairways and stoops laid by master crafters add distinctive detail and value. Custom-cut curved bluestone steps, hand selected by an experienced paving contractor, provide years of pride and pleasure.

Hardscape installation doesn't begin until your new home is nearly complete, but for your own budgeting purposes, have decisions made no later than home mid-construction phase.

To interview a paving or hardscape contractor, set up an on-site meeting so you can discuss the nature of the project and express your ideas. Be ready to answer questions like:

• Will the driveway be used by two or three cars, or more? Do you need it to be wide enough so cars can pass? Will you require extra parking? Would you like a circular driveway? A basketball court?

• Will the patio be used for entertaining? Will it be a family or adult area, or both? How much furniture will you use? Should it be accessible from a particular part of the house?

• Do you have existing or future landscaping that needs to be considered?

• Would you like to incorporate special touches, like a retaining wall or a stone archway?

If you're working with a full service landscape professional, and hardscape is part of the landscape design, be certain a hardscape expert will do the installation. A specialist's engineering expertise and product knowledge are vital to the top quality result you want. ■

SOURCES

American Society of Landscape Architects
636 Eye St., NW
Washington, DC 20001
202.898.2444
www.asla.org

Hardscape
Contractors

PREMIER DESIGNS ....**(713) 462-2525**
8302 Northcourt, Houston
See ad on page 163

Landscape
Architects

AJ'S LANDSCAPING & DESIGN, INC..**(713) 957-0449**
1223 West 21st Street, Houston   Fax:(713) 864-0842
See ad on page 169
Website: www.ajslandscaping.com
e-mail: aj@ajslandscaping.com

MASHUE'S LANDSCAPE & DESIGN, INC. ....**(713) 680-0658**
6121 Pinemont, Suite A, Houston   Fax:(713) 680-2355
See ad on page 164
e-mail: mashues@swbell.net

Landscape
Contractors

EXTERIOR WORLDS ....**(713) 827-2255**
See ad on page 154B, 154C, 165   Fax:(713) 461-3032

LEGACY LANDSCAPE MANAGEMENT, INC. ....**(281) 564-1500**
12999 Murphy Road, Ste. K, Stafford   Fax:(281) 564-3344
See ad on page 166, 167
Website: www.legacy-landscape.com
e-mail: john@legacy-landscape.com

MASHUE'S LANDSCAPE & DESIGN, INC. ....**(713) 680-0658**
6121 Pinemont, Suite A, Houston   Fax:(713) 680-2355
See ad on page 164
e-mail: mashues@swbell.net

PREMIER DESIGNS ....**(713) 462-2525**
8302 Northcourt, Houston
See ad on page 163

Landscape
Lighting

MASHUE'S LANDSCAPE & DESIGN, INC. ....**(713) 680-0658**
6121 Pinemont, Suite A, Houston   Fax:(713) 680-2355
See ad on page 164
e-mail: mashues@swbell.net

162

continued on page 170

Paradise Found

All Photos: Larry Fagala Photography

Let Mashue's create an *Eden* for you with our original outdoor designs that feature uncompromising quality workmanship, and finished with integrity and superb service.

LANDSCAPING
HARDSCAPES
WATER FEATURES
LIGHTING

A.S.L.A. LANDSCAPE ARCHITECT
POOLS AND SPAS
IRRIGATION
MAINTENANCE

Mashue's
LANDSCAPE DESIGN, INC.

SINCE 1988

713.680.0658

The creative process meshes your thoughts with our expertise. This is where we focus your ideas and ours into a cohesive look...and it is when our meticulous attention to detail and commitment to personal service truly shine.

Exterior Worlds

L A N D S C A P E

phone 7 1 3 . 8 2 7 . 2 2 5 5

Legacy

LANDSCAPE MANAGEMENT INC.

*Serving The Selective
Client Who Appreciates
Excellence*

Design · **Lighting**

Irrigation · **Drainage**

Hardscape · **Pools**

Mosquito Systems

Home Books

12 Tips
For Pursuing Quality

1. Assemble a Team of Professionals During Preliminaries.
Search out and value creativity.

2. Educate Yourself on What to Expect.
But also be prepared to be flexible in the likely event of setbacks.

3. Realize the Value and Worth of Design.
It's the best value for your investment.

4. Be Involved in the Process.
It's more personally satisfying and yields the best results.

5. Bigger Isn't Better – Better is Better.
Look for what produces quality and you'll never look back.

6. Understand the Process.
Be aware of products, prices and schedules, to be a productive part of the creative team.

7. Present a Realistic Budget.
Creative, workable ideas can be explored.

8. Create the Right Environment.
Mutual respect, trust and communication get the job done.

9. There Are No Immediate Miracles.
Time is a necessary component in the quest for quality.

10. Have Faith in Yourself.
Discover your own taste and style.

11. Plan for the Future.
Lifestyles and products aren't static.

12. Do Sweat the Details.
Establish the discipline to stay organized.

HOUSTON HOME BOOK

10900 Northwest Freeway, Suite 122, Houston, TX 77092   713.263.0471 FAX 713.263.1927

continued from page **162**

Lighting

ILLUMINATIONS LIGHTING DESIGN ....**(713) 863-1133**
607 Durham Drive, Houston   Fax:(713) 863-0044
See ad on page 147, 179
<u>Website:</u> www.illuminationslighting.com
<u>e-mail:</u> tom@illuminationslighting.com

Sport Facilities

GOLF TURFS OF HOUSTON ....**(713) 223-8873**
9909 Harwin, Ste. I, Houston
See ad on page 182

RHINO SPORTS OF HOUSTON ....**NORTHWEST: (713) 539-3248**
PO Box 820714, Houston   Southwest: (281) 293-0918
See ad on page 183   Fax:(713) 896-1711
<u>Website:</u> www.rhinocourts.com

SPORT COURT OF HOUSTON ....**(281) 242-4909**
935 Eldridge Rd., PMB 273, Sugar Land   Fax:(281) 242-1929
See ad on page 180, 181
<u>Website:</u> www.sportcourt.com
<u>e-mail:</u> claygivens@myexcel.com

Swimming Pools & Spas

ANTHONY & SYLVAN POOLS ....**(877) SAY-SWIM**
1424 W. Sam Houston Pkwy, Ste. 180, Houston   Fax:(713) 467-9135
See ad on page 154D
<u>Website:</u> www.anthonysylvan.com

FOX FAMILY POOLS...**(281) 550-7665**
See ad on page 177   (281) 446-5869
<u>Website:</u> www.foxfamilypools.com   Fax:(281) 446-6734

PINELOCH POOL CONSTRUCTION ....**(281) 461-4648**
626 1/2 Barringer Ln., Ste. A, Webster   Fax:(281) 480-7345
See ad on page 174, 175
<u>Website:</u> www.pinelochpools.com
<u>e-mail:</u> ppcc@swbell.net

PLATINUM POOLS..**(281) 870-1600**
410 Hwy 6 S. #F, Houston   Fax:(281) 870-1505
See ad on page 172, 173
<u>Website:</u> www.platinumpools.com
<u>e-mail:</u> scott@platinumpools.com

RICHARD'S TOTAL BACKYARD SOLUTIONS ....**(713) 468-8827**
1701 Highway 6 South, Houston   Fax:(281) 531-5623
See ad on page 178
<u>Website:</u> www.totalbackyardsolutions.com
<u>e-mail:</u> julie@totalbackyardsolutions.com

STARLIGHT POOLS ....**(281) 370-4711**
7822 Spring Cypress, Spring   Fax:(281) 320-1079
See ad on page 171
<u>Website:</u> www.starlightpools.com
<u>e-mail:</u> starlight-pools@sbcglobal.net

Pineloch Pool
Construction

Houston's Premier Pool Builder
Since 1983
281-461-4648
www.pinelochpools.com

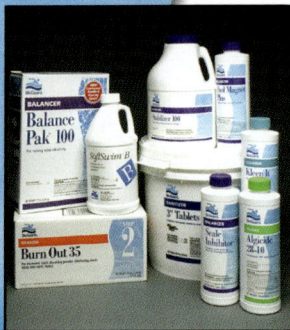

LANDSCAPE

Annual
A plant whose life cycle is completed in a single growing season - such as the snapdragon, ornamental cabbage and coleus.

Butterfly gardening
A process of selecting plants for the garden specifically to attract butterflies. Certain plants have different attractions for butterflies. "Host plants" draw mating pairs to lay eggs, and the resulting young caterpillars will consume the plant. "Nectar plants" create nectar, which attracts adult butterflies to feed.

Carpet bedding
Beds of small annual plants with ornamental foliage or flowers are arranged in patterns to be seen from above, such as from a deck or balcony. May include gravel sections or paths.

Disappearing edge pool
A pool with no visible coping or decking, blending into the surrounding and becoming a natural part of the landscape. The edges exist in the form of a catch basin to recycle the water back to the pool. Also known as a negative edge pool.

Fencerow
Planting which forms a fence or is adjacent to a fence.

Hardscape
The non-plant elements of a landscape. The term refers to hard elements such as those composed of wood, concrete, brick or stone. This includes pools, decks, patios, fences, retaining walls and other related landscape elements.

Herbaceous border
A permanent border of non-woody perennials, often against an evergreen background or a stone wall.

Herbaceous perennial
A plant that has no woody stem above ground. A non-woody plant that dies back to the ground each year.

Masonry
The art of shaping, arranging and uniting stone, brick, building blocks, etc. to form walls and other parts of a building.

Mulch
Material such as leaves, hay, straw, wood chips or the like, spread over the surface of the ground to protect the roots of newly planted shrubs or trees, or tender plants, from the sun or from the cold.

Perennial
A plant or shrub whose life cycle is greater than two years - such as the chrysanthemum, black-eyed susan and hibiscus.

Retaining wall
A wall or structure designed to prevent displacement of soil or other materials at a steeper slope than normal.

Softscape
This refers to the gardens, lawns, arbors and other planted areas of a landscape.

Woody perennial
The shrubs, trees or vines which do not die to the ground during winter.

Xeriscape
An attractive, sustainable landscape that conserves water and is based on sound horticultural practices.

KITCHEN

BATH

DAUPHIN SALES

Kitchen Remodeled by Valor Construction

SPECTRUM STONE, INC

Providing the highest quality fabrication
& installation of stone products

832.455.5132 ph
713.871.1054 fax

185

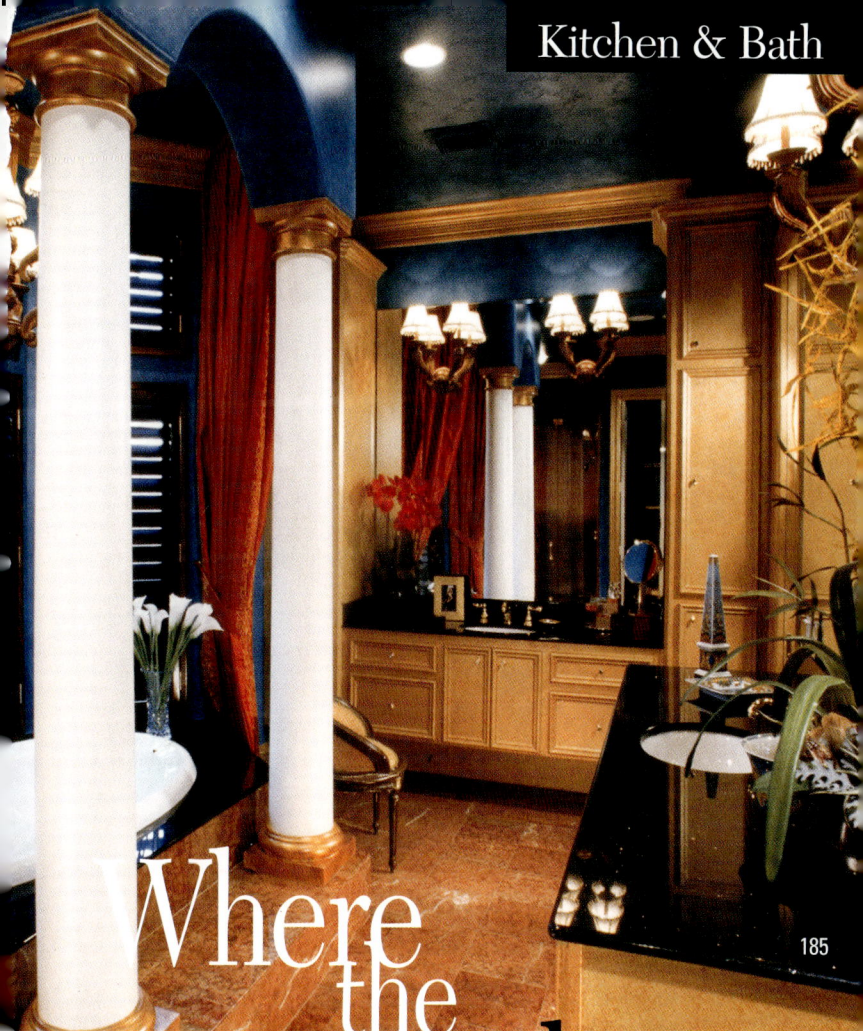

Where the Hearth Is

We've all seen the kitchen open up over the past few years, adding work stations and islands for seating, entertaining or food preparation. Kitchens today sport professional quality appliances and accessories, enabling the homeowners to store red wine at room temperature while chilling white wine, dispense draft beer at home and store and access food easily with new bottom mount freezer refrigerators.

Bathrooms, meanwhile, are better described as home spas today. The man and woman of the house can retreat to a quiet place of repose, and get dressed afterwards in their own private quarters.

Photo courtesy of **Hann Builders**
Photo by **John Blackmer**

DEFINING THE WAY WE LIVE

Homeowners building a new home, or remodeling an existing one, demand flexible and efficient spaces, custom designed to fill their needs. Reaching that goal is more challenging than ever. As new products and technologies race to keep up with the creative design explosion, the need for talented, experienced kitchen and bath designers continues to grow.

The kitchen/bath designer will be a member of your homebuilding team, which also includes the architect, contractor, interior designer and, in new home construction, the landscape architect.

Professional kitchen and bath designers, many of whom are also degreed interior designers, possess the education and experience in space planning particular to kitchens and baths. They can deliver a functional design perfectly suited to your family, while respecting your budget and your wishes. Their understanding of ergonomics, the relationship between people and their working environments, and a familiarity with current products and applications will be invaluable to you as you plan.

SEARCH OUT DESIGN EXCELLENCE

Designing a kitchen or bath is an intimate undertaking, filled with many decisions based on personal habits and family lifestyles. Before you select the kitchen/bath professional who will lead you through the project, make a personal commitment to be an involved and interested client. Since the success of these rooms is so important to the daily lives of you and those around you, it's a worthwhile investment of your time and energy.

Choose a designer whose work shows creativity and a good sense of planning. As in any relationship, trust and communication are the foundations for success. Is the designer open to your ideas, and does he or she offer information on how you can achieve your vision? If you can't express your ideas freely, don't enter into a contractual relationship, no matter how much you admire this person's work. If these rooms aren't conceived to fulfill your wishes, your time and resources will be wasted.

What also is true, however, is that professional designers should be given a comfortable degree of latitude to execute your wishes as best as they know how. Accomplished designers earned their reputation by creating beautiful rooms that work, so give their ideas serious consideration for the best overall result.

Many homeowners contact a kitchen or bath designer a year before a project is scheduled to begin. Some come with a full set of complete drawings they simply want to have priced out. Some take full

INGREDIENTS OF A NEW KITCHEN

What might it cost to design and install a 16 ft. x 33 ft. kitchen?
• **Cabinetry: kitchen, island, pantry, desk, 36-42 in. high wall cabinets, maple, modified Shaker styling, custom solid wood construction: $44,000**
• **Stained glass doors, glass shelves: $3,500**
• **Granite countertop & tumbled marble backsplash with mosaic: $14,500**
• **Two electric ovens, 36 in. gas cooktop with hood, 48 in. built-in refrigerator, two dishwashers, under counter refrigerator, warming drawer, microwave, disposal, hot water dispenser: $20,000**
• **Plumbing fixtures: $2,900**
• **Porcelain tile flooring: $4,000**
• **Lighting: low voltage, halogen and xenon: $2,500**
• **Labor: $7,000**
Total: $98,400

advantage of the designer's expertise and contract for plans drawn from scratch. And some want something in between. Be sure a designer offers the level of services you want – from 'soup to nuts' or strictly countertops and cabinetry.

Designers charge a design fee, which often will be used as a deposit if you choose to hire them. If you expect very detailed sets of drawings, including floor plans, elevations, and pages of intricate detail, such as the support systems of kitchen islands, the toe kick and crown molding detail, be specific about your requirements. All contracts should be written, detailed, and reviewed by your attorney.

TURNING DREAMS INTO DESIGNS – GET YOUR NOTEBOOK OUT

The first step toward getting your ideas organized is to put them on paper. Jot down notes, tape photos into an Idea Notebook, mark pages of your Home Book. The second step is defining your lifestyle. Pay close attention to how you use the kitchen and bath. For example, if you have a four-burner stove, how often do you cook with all four burners? Do you need a cook surface with more burners, or could you get by with less, freeing up space for a special wok cooking module or more counter space? How often do you use your bathtub? Many upper-end homeowners are forgoing the tub in favor of the multi-head shower surround and using bathtub space for a dressing or exercise area or mini-kitchen. As you evaluate your lifestyle, try to answer questions like these:

THINKING ABOUT KITCHEN DESIGN

• What feeling do you want to create in the kitchen? Traditional feel of hearth and home? The clean, uncluttered lines of contemporary design?

• Is meal preparation the main function of the kitchen? Gourmet cooks and gardeners want a different level of functionality than do homeowners who eat out often or want to be in and out of the kitchen quickly.

• How does the family use the kitchen? How will their needs change your requirements over the next ten years? (If you can't imagine the answer to this question, ask friends who are a few years ahead of you in terms of family life.)

• Do you want easy access to the backyard, dining room, garage?

• Is there a special view you want preserved or established?

APPLIANCES NOW

New appliances in the kitchen are fun and user-friendly.
• Prep sinks and cooktops located conveniently in the island
• Refrigerators with titanium finishes that don't leave fingerprints
• Monitors that can be built-in or mounted under a cabinet.
• Wireless water-proof keyboards for surfing the Internet while bathing or cooking
• Refrigerator touch screens for pulling up favorite recipes
• Dishwashers with a full-size, flat third rack for broiler pans, cook-ie sheets and other hard-to-wash items
• Recessed light-ing and task light-ing fixtures, such as sleek pendant lamps
• Built-in coffeemakers with electrical lift systems that hide them within a cab-inet after the lattes and espressos have been served.

1. Access to the newest products: With their considerable knowledge of products and solutions, your remodeling or budget limitations can be more easily addressed.

2. Ergonomic design for a custom fit: Designers consider all the measurements - not just floor plan space - but also how counter and cabinet height and depth measure up to the needs of the individual family members.

3. A safe environment: Safety is the highest priority. As kitchens and baths serve more functions, managing traffic for safety's sake becomes more crucial.

4. Orderly floor plans: When an open refrigerator door blocks the path from the kitchen to the breakfast room, or you're bumping elbows in the bathroom, poor space planning is the culprit.

5. Smart storage: Ample storage in close proximity to appropriate spaces is essential.

• Do you want family and friends to be involved and close to the action in the kitchen?

• What appliances and amenities must be included? Warming drawers, refrigeration zones, wine coolers, ultra-quiet dishwashers that sense how dirty the dishes are, cooktops with interchangeable cooking modules, and convection ovens with electronic touchpad controls are all available.

• What are your storage needs? If you own a lot of kitchen items, have a relatively small kitchen, or want personally tailored storage space, ask your kitchen designer to take a detailed inventory of your possessions. Top quality cabinets can be customized to fit your needs. Kitchen designers, custom cabinetmakers, or space organization experts can guide you. Consider custom options such as:
  • Slotted storage for serving trays
  • Pull-out recycling bins
  • Plate racks and wine racks
  • Cutlery dividers
  • Angled storage drawer for spices
  • Pivoting shelving systems
  • Pull-out or elevator shelves for food processors, mixers, televisions or computers

• Is the kitchen also a work area or home office? Do you need a location for a computerized home management or intercom system?

THINKING ABOUT BATH DESIGN

• What look are you trying to create? Victorian, Colonial, Contemporary, whimsical?

• What functions must it fill? Exercise area, sitting room, dressing or make-up area?

• Who will use the bath? Children, teens, guests (and how many)?

• What is the traffic pattern? How do people move in and around a bathroom? (Set up your video camera in the corner one morning to get a realistic view.)

• What amenities are desired? Luxury shower systems, whirlpool tub, ceiling heat lamps, spa, heated tile floors, audio and telephone systems

• What are your storage needs? Linen or clothes closets? Stereo and CD storage? Professionals will customize spaces for your needs.

• Do you want hooks for towels or bathrobes? Heated towel bars or rings?

THE SKY'S THE LIMIT

New high-end kitchen budgets can easily reach the $100,000 range, so it's important to identify your specific needs and wishes. The sky's the limit when designing and installing a luxury kitchen or bath in the 2000s, so don't get caught by surprise by the cost of high quality cabinetry, appliances and fixtures. Know what you're willing to spend and make sure your designer is aware of your budget. Projects have a way of growing along the way. If you've established a realistic budget, you have a solid way to keep the project moving forward and prioritizing your wishes. Think in terms of this general breakdown of expenses:

Cabinets 40%
Appliances 15%
Faucets and Fixtures 8%
Flooring 7%
Windows 7%
Countertops 8%
Labor 15%

TODAY'S KITCHEN-ANTIQUE OR SLEEK, IT'S YOUR CHOICE

Whether your tastes run to classical and traditional European designs, or you prefer contemporary looks, today's imperative is custom. You determine what you want. Gorgeous imported natural stone countertops and floors, and luxury options like dedicated wine coolers, stem glass holders, and plate racks are ever popular and can be accommodated in any style.

Today's refrigerators can now serve as home automation control centers. Plasma screens built into refrigerator doors can serve as touch-screen home automation control centers, running everything from ovens and entertainment centers to security systems. In other modes, they function as TV screens, even Internet portals. Check your e-mail while you're peeling the potatoes – why not!

With advances in refrigeration technology, homeowners now have separate integrated refrigerators and freezer drawers installed near the appropriate work zone – a refrigerated vegetable drawer near the sink, a freezer drawer by the microwave, dedicated refrigerators to keep grains or cooking oils at their perfect temperatures. Ultra-quiet dishwashers with push-button controls hidden on top of the door for a sleek appearance, instant hot water dispensers, roll-out warming drawers and cooktops that can boil water in seconds are just some of the products that meet the demands of today's luxury lifestyle.

"WHAT ABOUT RESALE?"

This is a question designers hear when homeowners individualize their kitchens and baths. It's only prudent to consider the practical ramifications of any significant investment, including investing in a new custom kitchen and bath.

Beautiful upscale kitchens and baths will only enhance the value of your home. Indeed, these two rooms are consistently credited with recouping more than their original cost, estimates range from an increase in value of 10% to 50% over what was spent. The greatest return, however, is in the present, in the enjoyment of the space.

TODAY'S BATH – BRINGING THE SPA EXPERIENCE HOME

Imagine it's a Thursday night at the end of a very busy week. You come home, have a great work out while listening to your favorite CDs over the loudspeakers in your private exercise room, then jump into an invigorating shower where multiple shower heads rejuvenate your tired muscles, and a steaming, cascading waterfall pulls all the stress from your body. You wrap yourself in a big fluffy bath sheet, toasty from the brass towel warmer as you step onto the ceramic tile floor that's been warmed by an underfloor radiant heating unit. You grab something comfortable from your lighted, walk-in closet, and then head out of your luxurious bathroom to the kitchen to help with dinner.

Today's master baths are indeed at-home spas. They are a place to de-stress from hectic and active lifestyles, and new designs seek to accomplish this through simplicity, softness of textures and surfaces, and the use of water's soothing nature itself. You've heard about aromatherapy, now there's "chromatherapy" – colored lights located in the bathtub. The system cycles through eights hues, and if you like a particular color, you can settle on that one by pushing a button.

For the utmost in minimalist faucet design, how about eliminating the faucet altogether? New faucet designs have the water flowing directly out of the wall. Used with porcelain hand basins, these wet surface lavatories are formulated for a comforting, almost Zen-like washing experience. Water flows onto a raised plateau, with an overflow perimeter reminiscent of disappearing edge pools that catches the water and sends it down the drain. The open-bottom hand basin creates a seal with the lavatory's surface when filled with water, enabling you to use it as a wash basin and then release the contents by simply lifting it. Perfect for those who want the experience of washing in a fountain instead of an ordinary sink.

For those seeking a mega-experience, spa tubs can provide the bathing equivalent of the Jumbotron. Watch a 48-inch color plasma TV screen as you pop in a video and soak to your heart's content (though soaking through a 3-hour movie like Lord of the Rings might be a bit much.)

THE REALITY OF REMODELING

Dollar-smart homeowners know that in cost versus value surveys, kitchen renovations and bath additions or renovations yield a very high return

---

A STEP UP

Custom counter height is an idea whose time has arrived in new and remodeled homes. Multiple heights, appropriate to the task or the people using the particular area, are common. When one permanent height doesn't work as a solution to a problem, consider asking for a step to be built in to the toe kick panel of the cabinetry.

GET TWO DISHWASHERS

Homeowners today are installing extra dishwashers:
1. To make cleanup after a party a one-night affair.
2. To serve as a storage cabinet for that extra set of dishes.
They're also installing dishwashers at a more friendly height to eliminate unnecessary bending.

on the original investment. These homeowners rarely embark on such remodeling projects with resale in mind. However, knowing their investment is a wise one gives them the freedom to fully realize their dreams of the ultimate sybaritic bath or the friendliest family kitchen that accommodates them now and well into the future.

For more information on remodeling, see "The Second Time's The Charm" in the Custom Home Builders and Remodelers section.

A REMODELING CONTINGENCY FUND

Kitchen and bath remodeling projects are well known for unexpected, unforeseen expenses, so put a contingency fund in your budget from the beginning. This fund can cover anything from structural changes to your sudden desire to install skylights in the kitchen.

THE BEAUTY OF TOP QUALITY SURFACES

Luxury surfaces continue to add astonishing beauty to kitchens and baths in new and remodeled homes throughout the area. Solid surfaces now are available in an ever-widening range of colors, including a granite look, with high degrees of translucence and depth. Granite and stone add a beautiful, natural look, with an abundance of choices and finishes. Tile, stainless steel, laminates, and wood – even concrete – are other possibilities. Each surface has its benefits, beyond the inherent beauty it can add to your design.

Your kitchen designer will advise you on the best choices for your project, based on overall design and budget. Use the professionals showcased in these pages to find the best quality materials and craftsmanship. ∎

ELECTRIC VS. GAS

An age-old debate, yes, but today's electric ranges have come a long way. Sleek, scratch-resistant glass cooktops feature simmer settings that hold sauces and stews below the boiling point. And controls can be locked for child-safety. Today's gas ranges feature grates that are dishwasher safe and sealed burners that make cleanup easy. Dual-stacked burners offer greater low-end control for melting or simmering. Electric, gas or both; the choice is yours.

191

Fixtures &
Hardware

DAUPHIN SALES, INC...**(713) 522-3418**
  8556 Katy Freeway, Suite 121, Houston   Fax:(713) 522-3467
  See ad on page 184B, 184C
  <u>Website:</u> www.dauphinsales.com
  <u>e-mail:</u> dauphin@swbell.net

Kitchen &
Bath Surfaces

BUILDERSPLUS ....**(281) 752-0693**
  1434 W. Sam Houston Pkwy N., Ste. 180, Houston   Fax:(281) 752-6236
  See ad on page 193
  <u>e-mail:</u> builderplus@aol.com

SPECTRUM STONE, INC ....**(832) 455-5132**
  Houston   Fax:(713) 871-1054
  See ad on page 184D
  <u>e-mail:</u> laurelber@yahoo.com

"Counter Options"

Silestone Natural Quartz - Granite - Travertine

Kitchen Counter Tops - Bathroom Vanities - Flooring - Shower Walls

Designers - Builders - Remodelers

BuildersPlus
"The Builder's First Choice!"

281.752.0693
fax 281.752.6236

SILESTONE
by Cosentino

DESIGN

The following design books represent the premier works of selected designers, luxury homebuilders and architects.

This book is divided into 10 chapters, starting with design guidelines in regard to color, personality and collections. In these chapters, interior designer Perla Lichi presents beautiful, four-color photographs of the design commissions she has undertaken for clients accompanied by informative editorial on the investment value of professional interior design.

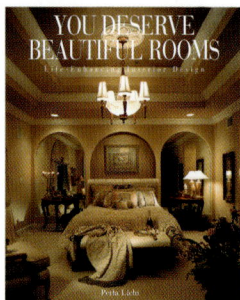

YOU DESERVE BEAUTIFUL ROOMS
120 pages, 9.75" x 14"
Home Design, Architecture
1-58862-016-6 $39.95   Hardcover

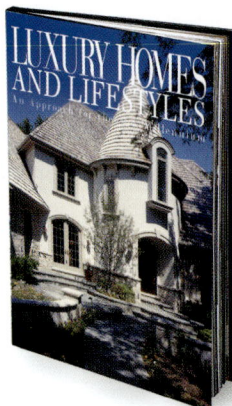

Orren Pickell is renowned as one of the nation's finest builders of custom homes. In this collection of more than 80 beautiful four-color photos and drawings, Pickell shows off some of his finest creations to give homeowners unique ideas on building a new home or adding to an existing one.

LUXURY HOMES & LIFESTYLES
120 pages, 9.75" x 14"
Architecture, Home Design
0-9642057-4-2 $39.95   Hardcover

Designer Susan Fredman has spent 25 years creating interiors, which, in one way or another, have been inspired by nature. In this book, she takes readers through rooms which reflect elements of our surroundings as they are displayed throughout the year.

AT HOME WITH NATURE
136 pages, 11.25" x 11.25"
Home Design, Architecture
1-58862-043-3 $39.95   Hardcover

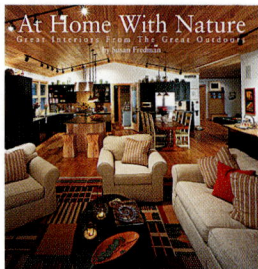

The Ashley Group is proud to present these speci

CALL TO ORDEF

BOOKS

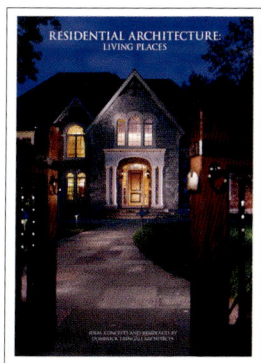

Michigan-based architect Dominick Tringali uses the skill and knowledge that has brought him over 20 industry awards to share strategies on building the ultimate dream house. By combining unique concepts with innovative techniques and materials, Dominick's portfolio displays an array of homes noted for their timeless appeal. This $45 million collection of elite, custom homes contains the residences of notable CEOs, lawyers, doctors and sports celebrities including Chuck O'Brien, Joe Dumars, Tom Wilson, Larry Wisne and Michael Andretti.

RESIDENTIAL ARCHITECTURE:
LIVING PLACES
144 pages
9" x 12"
Art & Architecture
1-58862-088-3
$39.95   Hardcover

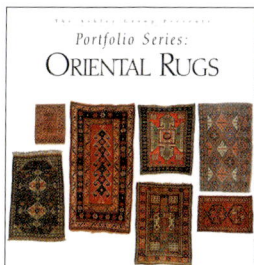

Top rug dealers throughout the country are profiled to provide helpful hints to successfully choose a rug that best suits a buyer's needs. Readers will also gain an understanding of the key elements to consider when purchasing an Oriental rug. Over 100 images will help a potential buyer get a feel for the styles and patterns available through each dealer. Additionally, this book provides a solid directory of vendors who hold invaluable expertise in this arena.

PORTFOLIO SERIES:
ORIENTAL RUGS
July 2003
150 pages
10" x 10"
Home Design
1-58862-987-2
$29.95   Hardcover

les on luxury home style, design and architecture
888.458.1750

KITCHEN & BATH

Backsplash
A protective panel on the wall behind a sink or counter.

Base Molding
Molding used to trim the upper edge of interior baseboards.

Fume Hood
A partial enclosure through which air is drawn to remove gases and odors within the enclosed area. Usually above the stove in the kitchen.

Toekick (also called Toeboard)
A recessed face of a cabinet, at toe level.

Refrigerated drawer
A small, refrigerated storage unit located directly under the counter top. This is especially convenient during food preparation or for beverage storage.

Seamless sink
A single sink and counter unit, therefore lacking in seams between the two elements.

Work triangle
The kitchen area from the refrigerator to the main cooking area to the main sink. The three together should form a triangular layout. At or immediately adjacent to the triangle's points is where all the all the key kitchen activities take place.

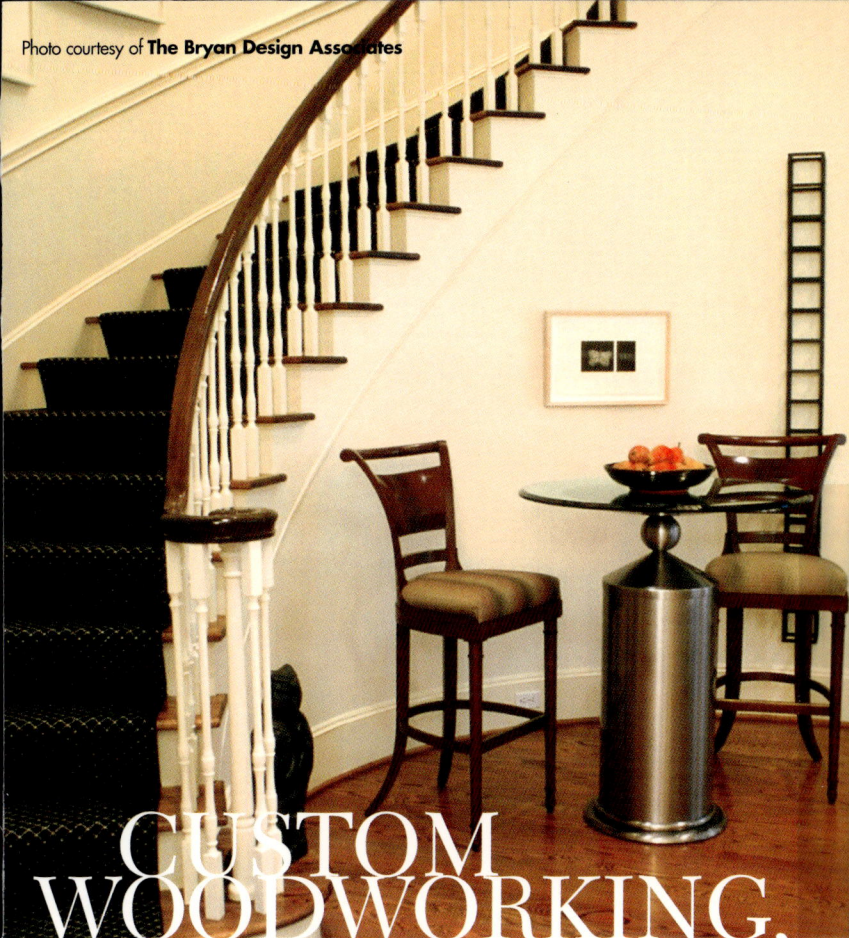

Photo courtesy of **The Bryan Design Associates**

CUSTOM WOODWORKING, METALWORKING, HARDWARE & GLASS

BUILDING MATERIALS, LTD.

The preeminent resource
for residential construction materials
in the Greater Houston area.

Please visit
our showrooms
located at:

Houston
1445 West Sam Houston
Parkway North
713.467.6700

The Woodlands
15585 I-45 South
Conroe, TX 77385
713.935.1245

Visit us on the Web at
www.bisonbuilding.com

197

Masterworks
of
Detail

W hat better way to make a home unique than to employ the talents of a master craftsman? Want a shower that's bordered in block glass? Perhaps a stained glass window in the foyer? Today's craftsmen will yield results that give a unique flair to your home, whether they are installing an exotic, carved walnut fireplace or hammering out wrought iron balustrade components for the staircase. These delicate touches provide charm and grace to any home.

Photo courtesy of **Hann Builders**
Photo by **John Blackmer**

ELEGANT STORAGE

Nowhere is the commitment to elegant living through quality materials more apparent than in the selection of cabinets and millwork. Representing a significant percentage of the overall cost of a new or renovated home, sophisticated homeowners use this opportunity to declare their dedication to top quality.

Architectural millwork, made to order according to a set of architectural drawings, is becoming an increasingly popular luxury upgrade. Such detailing creates a richly nostalgic atmosphere that reminds homeowners of the comfort and security of a grandparents' home or the elegance of a club they've been in.

Elegant libraries, dens or sitting rooms dressed with fashionable raised panel cabinetry and special moldings are often included in the plans for new homes and remodeling projects. As a homeowner considering how and where to install millwork, ask yourself questions like these:

• How is the room used? Will a study be used for work or for solitude? Entertaining or a second office? Will it have to function as both a working office and an elegant room?

• How are the cabinets and shelves used? Books, collectibles, audio-video equipment, computer, fax or copy machines?

• What look do you want? You may want to consider "dressing" your rooms in different woods. You may like the rich look and feel of cherry paneling in your library, mahogany in the foyer, oak in a guest room and plaster in a dining room.

• Will the interior millwork choices work with the exterior architecture? A colonial home reminiscent of Mount Vernon should be filled with authentic details, like "dog-ear" corners, that create classic luxury. Using millwork inside a modern home can add interest and warmth to one or many rooms.

TAKE TIME TO MAKE A STATEMENT

Handcrafted high quality woodwork cannot be rushed. Millwork specialists encourage clients to contact them as early as possible with a clear idea of what kind of architectural statement they wish to make. The earlier you plan these details, the more options you'll have. Wainscoting with raised panels has to be coordinated with electrical outlets, window and door openings; beamed ceilings with light fixtures, and crown moldings with heating vents.

Hold a preliminary meeting before construction begins while it's early enough to incorporate innovative

---

PRICING A POWER LIBRARY

• A 15 ft. x 16 ft. library, fully paneled in cherry, mahogany or oak, some cabinets, with moldings, desk with hidden computer, coffered ceilings: $20,000 to $30,000.

• In a 16 ft. x 24 ft. two-story study, less paneling and more cabinetry of cherry, mahogany or oak, heavy with moldings, and radius work, desk with more pull out and hidden compartments for fax machine, small copier, bar with leaded glass cabinet fronts and a marble top, built-in humidor, and heavily coffered ceilings with multiple steps: $40,000.

198

HOW TO RECOGNIZE CUSTOM CABINET QUALITY

1. Proper sanding which results in a smooth, beautiful finish.
2. Superior detail work, adding unexpected elegance.
3. Classic application of design features and architectural details.
4. Beautiful, functional hardware selections.
5. High-quality hinges and drawer glides.
6. Superior overall functionality.

or special requirements into your plans. The more time you can devote to design (two to three weeks is recommended), the better your result will be. You're creating a custom millwork package that's never been designed for anyone before. Investments made on the front end are the most valuable. Ask about design fees, timelines and costs per revision. Keep your builder up to date on all of your millwork plans.

Drawings can be as detailed as you require. If you want to see the intricacies of a radius molding before you contract for it, let the millwork specialist know your requirements. Ask to see wood samples, with and without stain or paint.

Try to visit installed projects to get a firsthand feel for the quality of a specialist's work and to develop clearer ideas for your own home.

Changes made after an order is placed are costly. Therefore, if you're unsure, don't make a commitment. Add accessory moldings and other details as you see the project taking shape.

Expect a heavily laden room to take at least five to eight weeks to be delivered, about the time from the hanging of drywall to the installation of flooring. Installation takes one to three weeks, depending on the size and scope of the project.

THE SIGNATURE STATEMENT OF CUSTOM CABINETRY

Handcrafted custom cabinets are a recognizable standard of excellence which lend refinement and beauty to a home. Built in a kitchen, library, bathroom, or closet, or as a freestanding entertainment system or armoire, custom cabinets are a sophisticated signature statement.

DESIGNING HANDSOME CABINETRY

Cabinetry is a major element in your dream home, so let your imagination soar. Collect pictures of cabinets, noting the particular features you like. Cabinet makers appreciate visual examples because it's easier to interpret your desires from pictures than from words. Pictures crystallize your desires.

When you first meet with a cabinet maker, take your blueprints, and if possible, your builder, architect or designer. Be prepared to answer questions like:

• What is the exterior style of your home and do you want to continue that style inside?

• How will you the use the cabinets? Cutlery trays, pullout bins? Shelves for books, CDs, computer software, collections?

WHY YOU WANT A PROFESSION-AL DESIGNER

• They rely on experience to deliver you a custom product. Computer tools are great, but nothing replaces the experienced eye.
• They have established relationships with other trades, and can get top-quality glass fronts for your cabinets, or granite for a bar top.
• Their design ability can save you significant dollars in installation.
• They know how to listen to their clients and help them get the results they dream of.

199

PRICING OF CUSTOM KITCHEN CABINETS

• Deluxe Kitchen - Face frame-style cabinets of oak, maple or pine, with raised panel doors; crown molding on upper cabinetry, decorative hardware, wood nosing (cap) around counter tops: $10,000 - $20,000
• Upgrade to - Shaker inset-style cabinets in cherry-wood, painted finish: $20,000 additional.

- What styles and embellishments do you like? Shaker, Prairie, Country English, Contemporary? Fancy moldings, wainscoting, inlaid banding?

- Do you prefer particular woods? Cherry, oak, sycamore, or the more exotic ebony, Bubinga or Swiss pearwood? (Species must be selected on the basis of the finish you want.)

- Will cabinetry be visible from other rooms in the house? Must it match previously installed or selected flooring or countertops? (Take samples.)

MANAGING THE LENGTHY PROCESS OF A CUSTOM CABINET PROJECT

With plenty of unhurried time, you can be more creative, while allowing the woodworkers the time they need to deliver a top quality product. Take your blueprints to a cabinet maker early. Although installation occurs in the latter part of the construction, measuring usually takes place very early on.

If your project is carefully thought out, you won't be as likely to change your mind, but a contingency budget of 10 to 15 percent for changes (like adding radiuses or a lacquered finish) is recommended.

Custom cabinets for a whole house, (kitchen, butler's pantry, library, master bath, and three to four additional baths) may take 10 to 15 weeks, depending on the details involved (heavy carving adds significant time). Cabinets for a kitchen remodeling may take two months.

EXCEPTIONAL STAIRCASES

Take full advantage of the opportunity to upgrade your new or remodeled home with a spectacular staircase by contacting the stairmakers early in the design phase. Their familiarity with products, standards and building codes will be invaluable to you and your architect, contractor or interior designer.

Visit a stair showroom or workroom on your own or with your architect, interior designer or builder during the architectural drawing phase of your project. Discuss how you can achieve what you want at a cost-conscious price. Choosing a standard size radius of 24 inches, in place of a custom 25 ½ inch radius, for example, will help control costs.

Although your imagination may know no bounds in designing a staircase, hard and fast local building codes may keep your feet on the ground. Codes are not static, and stairmakers constantly update their files on local restrictions regarding details like the rise and run of a stair, and the size and height of rails.

USING PLASTER DETAILING

Plaster architectural detailing and trim add a distinctive look to any home. Most often used in out-of-the-way places, like in ceiling medallions or crown moldings, the high relief detailing is especially impressive.

PRICES OF CUSTOM STAIRS

Stairs can cost anywhere from $200 to $95,000, depending on size, materials and the complexity of design:
- **Red Oak spiral staircase, upgraded railing: $10,000**
- **Red Oak circle stairs, standard railings on both sides and around upstairs landing: $13,000**
- **Six flights of Red Oak circle stairs stacked one atop the next, with landings at the top of each stair: $95,000**
- **Walnut or mahogany adds 50 percent to the overall cost.**

THE STAIR-BUILDING PROCESS

The design of your stairs should be settled in the rough framing phase of the overall building project. If you work within this time frame, the stairs will be ready for installation after the drywall is hung and primer has been applied to the walls in the stair area.

Stairs can be built out of many woods. The most popular choice is red oak, but cherry, maple, walnut and mahogany are also used. If metal railings are preferred, you'll need to contact a specialist.

A top quality stair builder will design your stairs to your specifications. Consider the views you want of the house while on the stairs, and what kind of front entrance presentation you prefer. You may want to see the stairs from a particular room. An expert also can make suggestions regarding comfort and safety, and what styles will enhance the overall architecture.

Plans that are drawn on a computer can be changed with relative ease and can be printed at full size. This is very helpful to homeowners who want to see exactly what the stairs will look like in their home. The full-size plans can be taken to the job site and tacked to the floor to be experienced firsthand.

LOOKING AT THE BEAUTY OF CUSTOM GLASS AND MIRROR

A room can be transformed through the use of custom decorative glass and mirrors. Artists design intricately patterned, delicately painted glass to add light and architectural interest in all kinds of room dividers and partitions. Glass artistry can be based on any design, playing on the texture of carpet, the pattern of the brick, or repeating a fabric design. A glass block wall or floor panel can add the touch of distinction that sets a home above the others. Stained glass, usually associated with beautiful classic styling, can be designed in any style – from contemporary to art deco to traditional.

Top specialists, like those presented in the following pages, take great care in designing and delivering unique, top quality products. They work with top quality fabricated products, with the highest quality of beveling and edge work.

THE ARTISTIC PROCESS

Glass specialists will visit your home or building site to make recommendations and estimate costs and delivery time. Study their samples and if they have a showroom, go take a look. Perhaps you could visit an installed project. Seeing the possibilities can stimulate your imagination and open your eyes to new ideas in ways pictures simply cannot.

DOOR #1, #2, OR #3?

- Door #1 - Six panel oak door with sidelights of leaded glass: $1,700 - $2,000
- Door #2 - Six panel oak door with lead and beveled glass: $3,000
- Door #3 - Oversized, all matched oak, with custom designed leaded glass and brass, sidelights, elliptical top over door: $15,000
- Allow $500 to $1,500 for door-knobs, hinges and other hardware.

201

LUXURY GLASS & MIRROR

- **Mirrored Exercise Room: Floor to ceiling, wall to wall mirrors, on two or three walls. Allow at least a month, from initial measuring, to squaring off and balancing walls, to installation. Price for polished mirror starts around $9 per square foot. Cutouts for vent outlets cost extra.**
- **Custom Shower Doors: Frameless, bent or curved shower doors are popular luxury upgrades. Made of clear or sandblasted heavy glass - 1/2 in. to 3/8 in. thick. $2,000 and up.**
- **Stained Glass Room Divider: Contemporary, clear on clear design, with a hint of color. Approximately 4 ft. x 6 ft., inset into a wall. $4,500.**
- **Glass Dining Table: Custom designed with bevel edge, 48 in. x 96 in. with two glass bases. $1,200.**

Allow a month to make a decision and four weeks for custom mirror work delivery, and ten to 14 weeks for decorated glass.

In order to have the glass or mirror ready for installation before the carpet is laid, decisions must be made during the framing or rough construction phase in a new home or remodeling job. Mirrored walls are installed as painting is being completed, so touch-ups can be done while painters are still on site.

Expect to pay a 50 percent deposit on any order after seeing a series of renderings and approving a final choice. Delivery generally is included in the price.

THE BEAUTY AND CHARM OF CUSTOM WINDOWS AND DOORS

Just as we're naturally drawn to establish eye contact with each other, our attention is naturally drawn to the "eyes" of a home, the windows, skylights and glass doors.

These very important structural features, when expertly planned and designed, add personality and distinction to your interior while complementing the exterior architectural style of your home.

After lumber, windows are the most expensive part of a home. Take the time to investigate the various features and qualities of windows, skylights and glass doors. Visit a specialty store offering top of the line products and service and take advantage of their awareness of current products as well as their accumulated knowledge.

Visit a showroom with your designer, builder or architect. Because of the rapidly changing requirements of local building codes, it's difficult for them to keep current on what can be installed in your municipality. In addition, the dizzying pace of energy efficiency improvements over the past five years can easily outrun the knowledge of everyone but the window specialist. Interior designers can help you understand proper placement and scale in relation to furnishings and room use.

As you define your needs ask questions about alternatives or options, such as energy efficiency, ease of maintenance, appropriate styles to suit the exterior architecture, and interior.

Top quality windows offer high-energy efficiency, the best woodwork and hardware, and comprehensive service and guarantees (which should not be prorated). Good service agreements cover everything, including the locks.

Every home of distinction deserves an entry that exudes a warm welcome and a strong sense of homecoming. When we think of "coming home," we envision an entry door first, the strong, welcoming look of it, a first impression of the home behind it. To get the best quality door, contact a door or millwork specialist with a reputation for delivering top quality products. They can educate you on functionality, and wood and size choices and availability, as well as appropriate style. Doors are also made of steel or fiberglass, but wood offers the most flexibility for custom design.

Since doors are a permanent part of your architecture, carefully shop for the design that best reflects the special character of your home. Allow two to three weeks for delivery of a simple door and eight to 12 weeks if you're choosing a fancy front door. Doors are installed during the same phase as windows, before insulation and drywall.

DESIGN FLAIR HINGES ON FANTASTIC HARDWARE

Door and cabinet hardware, towel bars and accessories add style and substance to interiors. Little things truly do make the difference – by paying attention to the selection of top quality hardware in long-lasting, great-looking finishes, you help define your signature style and commitment to quality in a custom home. There are hundreds of possibilities, so when you visit a specialty showroom, ask the sales staff for their guidance. They can direct you towards the products that will complement your established design style and help you stay within the limits of your budget. When a rim lock for the front door can easily cost $500, and knobs can be $10 each, the advice of a knowledgeable expert is priceless.

Most products are readily available in a short time frame, with the exception of door and cabinetry hardware. Allow eight weeks for your door hardware, and three to four weeks for cabinetry selections. Since accessory hardware is usually in stock, changing cabinet knobs, hooks and towel bars is a quick and fun way to get a new look.

If you're looking to add a creative touch, black-smithing as decorative art has come to the fore as a way for homeowners to express their personal style. Whether reproductions of period pieces or a new, original design, ornamental iron combines strong, functional purpose with graceful art. ■

THREE TIPS FOR DOOR HARDWARE

1. Use three hinges to a door - it keeps the door straight.
2. Match all hardware - hinges, knobs, handles, all in the same finish. Use levers or knobs - don't mix.
3. Use a finish that will last.

203

Custom
Cabinets

JIM FARRIS CABINETS ....**(713) 947-2153**
2950 S. Shaver, #E-10, Pasadena   Fax:(713) 947-2175
See ad on page 196D
Website: www.farriscabinets.com
e-mail: jim@farriscabinets.com

Custom
Woodworking

BISON BUILDING MATERIALS LTD ....**(713) 467-6700**
1445 W. Sam Houston Pkwy., Houston   Fax:(713) 935-1224
See ad on page 196B, 196C
Website: www.bisonbuilding.com

QUALITY MILLWORK ....**(713) 723-5244**
11328 South Post Oak #202, Houston   Fax:(713) 723-5244
See ad on page 205

Hardware

SETTLERS HARDWARE ....**(713) 524-2417**
1901 West Alabama, Houston   Fax:(713) 524-4938
See ad on page 207
Website: www.settlershardware.com
e-mail: settlershardware@aol.com

QUALITY MILLWORK
Building On Experience & Quality

• Kitchens • Entertainment Centers
• Bathrooms • Bookcases • Home Office
• Architectural Cabinets & Furniture
• China Cabinets & Hutches

Houston's Premier
Home & Design
Sourcebook

The **Houston Home Book** is your final destination when searching for home remodeling, building and decorating resources. This comprehensive, hands-on sourcebook to building, remodeling, decorating, furnishing and landscaping a luxury home is required reading for the serious and discriminating homeowner. With more than 300 full-color, beautiful pages, the **Houston Home Book** is the most complete and well-organized reference to the home industry. This hardcover volume covers all aspects of the process, includes listings of hundreds of industry professionals, and is accompanied by informative and valuable editorial discussing the most recent trends. Ordering your copy of the **Houston Home Book** now can ensure that you have the blueprints to your dream home, in your hand, today.

Order your copy now!

HOUSTON
HOME
BOOK

Published by
The Ashley Group
10900 Northwest Freeway, Suite 122, Houston, TX 77092
713.263.0471 fax 713.263.1927
E-mail: ashleybooksales@reedbusiness.com

Settlers Hardware

The finishing touch for fine furniture and cabinetry

1901 W. Alabama Houston, Tx

713-524-2417

settlershardware.com

CUSTOM METAL,
WOODWORKING & GLASS

Coffering
Ceiling with deeply recessed panels, often highly ornamented.

Crown molding
Any molding serving as a corona or otherwise forming the crowning or finishing member of a structure.

Dovetail
A splayed projection end on a piece of wood shaped like a dove's tail, broader at its end than at the base. It forms a joint when fitted into the recesses of a corresponding piece.

Enriched
Having embellishment.

Engaged column
A column partially built into the wall, as opposed to freestanding.

Entablature
An elaborate horizontal band and molding supported by columns divided into three orders architrave, frieze, and cornice. The amount and style of detailing differs for each element.

...pi
A spire-shaped decorative element at the terminus of a projecting point or angle of a roof.

Imbrication
Overlapping rows of shaped tiles or shingles that resemble overlapping fish scales.

Knotwork
Carved ornamental arrangement of cord-like images knotted together, used to decorate moldings and trims.

Millwork
Ready-made products which are manufactured at a wood-planing mill or woodworking plant moldings, doors, door frames, window sashes, stair work, cabinets, etc.

Mosaic
A pattern formed by inlaying small pieces of stone, tile, glass or enamel into a cement, mortar, or plaster matrix.

Necking
A molding or group of moldings between a column and capital.

Trayed Ceiling
An elevated ceiling further recessed one or more times, creating tiers as the recessions move inward, finalizing in a wide, flat expanse of ceiling that is considerably higher than the starting level. It may also have strips of molding along or between each tier.

FLOORING

&

COUNTERTOPS

Come visit our showroom first...

The Gallery of Floors

FLOOR DESIGNERS
Signature Store

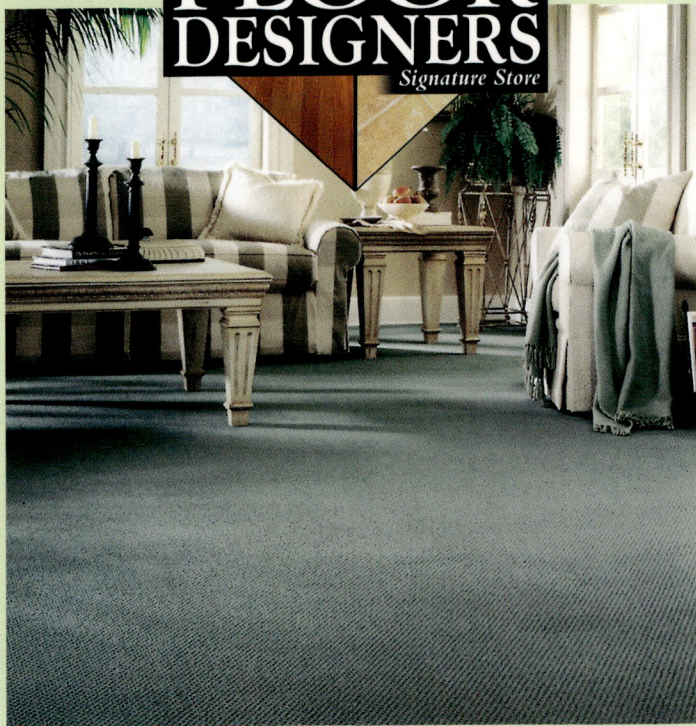

Call for a free estimate!

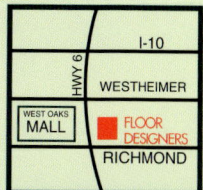

Beyond the Surface

The global village that is the world community today has opened up a variety of choices in surfaces for the homeowner. Exotic woods such as Brazilian cherry, Australian jarrah or Chinese bamboo are adding panache to many custom built homes. Concrete and stone floors are offering even more variety, especially in warm climates where a floor that's cool to the touch is welcome. Countertops, too, are experiencing an explosion in new materials, as manmade surfaces, concrete, and metals such as zinc and aluminum are added to the palette alongside the more traditional granite.

Photo by **Roland Bishop Photography**

DISTINGUISHED FLOOR COVERINGS... CARPETS & RUGS

From a room-sized French Aubusson rug to a dense wool carpet with inset borders, "soft" floor treatments are used in area homes to make a signature statement, or blend quietly into the background to let other art and furnishings grab the attention.

Selecting carpeting and rugs requires research, a dedicated search, and the guidance of a well-established design plan. Because the floor covers the width and depth of any room, it's very important that your choices are made in concert with other design decisions – from furniture to art, from window treatments to lighting.

Your interior designer or a representative at any of the fine retail stores featured in the following pages is qualified to educate you as you make your selections.

Rug and carpet dealers who cater to a clientele that demands a high level of personal service (from advice to installation and maintenance) and top quality products, are themselves dedicated to only the best in terms of service and selection. Their accumulated knowledge will be a most important benefit as you select the right carpet for your home.

THE WORLD AT YOUR FEET

Today's profusion of various fibers, colors, patterns, textures, and weights make carpet selection exciting and challenging. Your search won't be overwhelming if you realize the requirements of your own home and work within those boundaries.

Begin where the carpet will eventually end up – that is, in your home. Consider how a carpet will function by answering questions like these:

• What is the traffic pattern? High traffic areas, like stairs and halls, require a stain resistant dense or low level loop carpet for top durability in a color or pattern that won't show wear. Your choices for a bedroom, where traffic is minimal, will include lighter colors in deeper plush or velvets.

• How will it fit with existing or developing decors? Do you need a neutral for an unobtrusive background, or an eye-catching tone-on-tone texture that's a work of art in itself?

• Will it flow nicely into adjoining rooms? Carpet or other flooring treatments in the surrounding rooms need to be considered.

• What needs, other than decorative, must the carpet fill? Do you need to keep a room warm, muffle sound, protect a natural wood floor?

ORIENTAL RUGS

The decision to invest in an Oriental rug should be made carefully. Buying a rug purely for its decorative beauty and buying for investment purposes require two different approaches. If you're buying for aesthetics, put beauty first and condition second. Certain colors and patterns are more significant than others; a reputable dealer can guide you. Check for quality by looking at these features:
• Regularity of knotting.
• Color clarity.
• Rug lies evenly on the floor.
• Back is free of damage or repair marks.

BEYOND TRADITIONAL

Solid surfacing is now being used to make custom faucets, decorative wall tiles, and lots of other creative touches for the home. Their rich colors (including granite), famed durability and versatility are perfect for bringing ideas to life. Check with your countertop supplier for information and ideas.

• How is the room used? Do teenagers and toddlers carry snacks into the family room? Is a finished basement used for ping-pong as well as a home office?

THE ARTISTRY OF RUGS

N othing compares to the artful elegance of a carefully selected area rug placed on a hard surface. Through pattern, design, texture and color, rug designers create a work of art that is truly enduring. If you have hardwood, marble or natural stone floors, an area rug will only enhance their natural beauty. From Chinese silk, to colorful Pakistanis, to rare Caucasian antiques, the possibilities are as varied as the world is wide.

If you're creating a new interior, it's best to start with rug selection. First, it's harder to find the "right" rug than it is to find the "right" fabric or paint: there are simply fewer fine rugs than there are fabrics, patterns or colors. However, don't make a final commitment on a rug until you know it will work with the overall design. Second, rugs usually outlive other furnishings. Homeowners like to hang on to their rugs when they move, and keep them as family heirlooms.

In recent years, many rug clients have been enjoying a bounty of beautiful, well-made rugs from every major rug-producing country in the world. As competition for the global market intensifies, rugs of exceptionally high caliber are more readily available. Getting qualified advice is more important than ever.

Fine rug dealers, like those showcased in the following pages, have knowledgeable staff members who are dedicated to educating their clientele and helping them find a rug they'll love. Through careful consideration of your tastes, and the requirements of your home, these professionals will virtually walk you through the process. They'll encourage you to take your time, and to judge each rug on its own merits. They'll insist on you taking rugs home so that you can experience them in your own light (and may also provide delivery). And their companies will offer cleaning and repair service, which may well be important to you some day.

WARMING UP TO HARDWOOD

A hardwood floor is part of the dream for many custom homeowners searching for a warm, welcoming environment. Highly polished planks or fine parquet, the beauty of wood has always been a definitive part of luxurious homes and as the design "warming trend" continues, a wood floor figures prominently in achieving this feeling.

FOR SUCCESSFUL CARPET SHOPPING

1. Take along blueprints (or accurate measurements), fabric swatches, paint chips & photos.
2. Focus on installed, not retail price.
3. Take samples home to experience it in the light of the room.
4. Be aware of delivery times; most carpet is available within weeks; special orders or custom designs take much longer.
5. Shop together. It saves time in the decision-making process.

211

With new product options that make maintenance even easier, wood floors continue to add value and distinction in upscale homes throughout the area and the suburbs. Plank, parquet, and strip wood come in a wide variety of materials, and scores of styles and tones. Consider what effect you're trying to achieve.

Plank wood complements a traditional interior, while parquet wood flooring offers a highly stylized look. Designs stenciled directly on to floorboards create an original Arts and Crafts feel.

Brazilian cherry wood and tumbled travertine quarried from Italy are simply more accessible today, and the door is open to previously obscure materials such as Australian jarrah eucalyptus or American antique red heart cypress (also known as tidewater or bald cypress).

VINYL AND LAMINATES

Vinyl or laminated floor coverings are no longer considered candidates for immediate rehab. As a matter of fact, they're among the most updated looks in flooring. Stylish laminates are made to convincingly simulate wood, ceramic tile and other natural flooring products, and are excellent choices for heavy traffic areas. They come in hundreds of colors and patterns, and offer great compatibility with countertop materials.

THE RENAISSANCE OF CERAMIC TILE

Ceramic tile has literally come out of the back rooms and into the spotlight with its color, beauty and unique stylistic potential. As sophisticated shoppers gain a better understanding of the nature and possibilities of tile, its use has increased dramatically. Homeowners who want added quality and value in their homes are searching out hand painted glazed tiles for the risers of a staircase, quirky rectangular tiles to frame a powder room mirror, and ceramic tiles that look exactly like stone for their sun porch or kitchen. From traditional to modern, imported to domestic, ceramic tile offers a world of possibilities.

It is the perfect solution for homeowners who want floor, walls, countertops or backsplashes made of top quality, durable and attractive materials. A glazed clay natural product, ceramic tile is flexible, easy to care for, and allows for a variety of design ideas. It is easily cleaned with water and doesn't require waxing or polishing. And, like other natural flooring and counter products, ceramic tile adds visible value to a luxury home.

BUDGETING FOR WOOD FLOOR

- 2 ¼ in. strip oak - $10/sq. ft. Wider plank or parquet, glued & nailed - $15/sq. ft. Fancy parquet, hand-finished plank or French patterns (Versailles, Brittany) - $30/sq. ft. and up.
- Estimates include finishing and installation; not sub-floor trim.

212

THE NUMBER ONE WAY TO DECIDE ON A RUG

Do you like the rug enough to decorate around it? There's your answer.

SELECTING CERAMIC TILE

Not all tile works in all situations, so it's imperative that you get good advice and counsel when selecting ceramic tile for your home. Ceramic tile is wear-rated, and this standardized system will steer you in the right direction. Patronize specialists who can provide creative, quality-driven advice. Visit showrooms to get an idea of the many colors, shapes and sizes available for use on floors, walls and counters. You'll be in for a very pleasant surprise.

If you're building or remodeling, your builder, architect, and/or interior designer can help you in your search and suggest creative ways to enliven your interior schemes. Individual hand-painted tiles can be interspersed in a solid color backsplash to add interest and individuality. Tiles can be included in a glass block partition, on a wallpapered wall, or in harmony with an area rug.

Grout, which can be difficult to keep clean, is now being addressed as a potential design element. By using a colored grout, the grout lines become a contrast design element – or can be colored to match the tile itself.

THE SOPHISTICATED LOOK OF NATURAL STONE

For a luxurious look that radiates strength and character, the world of natural stone offers dazzling possibilities. As custom buyers look for that "special something" to add to the beauty and value of their homes, they turn to the growing natural stone marketplace. A whole world of possibilities is now open to involved homeowners who contact the master craftsmen and suppliers who dedicate their careers to excellence in stone design, installation and refurbishing.

Marble and granite, which have always been options for homeowners, are more popular than ever. With luxurious texture and color, marble is often the choice to add dramatic beauty to a grand entryway or a master bath upgrade. Granite continues to grow in popularity especially in luxury kitchens – there is no better material for countertops. It's also popular for a section of countertop dedicated to rolling pastry or dough. Rustic, weathered and unpolished, or highly polished and brilliant, granite brings elegance and rich visual texture that adds easily recognizable value to a home. Beyond marble and granite, the better suppliers of stone products also can introduce homeowners to slates, soapstone, limestone, English Kirkstone, sandstone, and travertine, which can be finished in a variety of individual ways.

DON'T GET COLD FEET

Stone and tile floors are known for their chilly feel. Electrical products are available now to help warm the surfaces of natural products. Installed in the adhesive layer under the flooring, these warming units are available at the better suppliers and showrooms.

CERAMIC TILE AS STONE

With textured surfaces and color variations, ceramic tile can look strikingly like stone. You can get the tone on tone veining of marble, or the look of split stone, in assorted shapes, sizes and color.

PRICING FOR NATURAL STONE

As with all flooring and countertop materials, get an installed, not a retail quote. Installation can drive the cost up significantly. Preparing a realistic quote may take days of research, due to the tremendous variety of factors that can influence price. As a general guideline, the installed starting price per square foot:

- Granite: $30
- Tumbled marble, limestone, slate: $20
- Engineered stone/quartzite: $25
- Antique stone, with intricate installation: $75
- Granite slab countertop: $70

SOLID SURFACING SHOWS UP ON TILES

Durable, nonporous solid surface materials are now being used to make decorative wall tiles. Check with your countertop supplier for information and ideas.

BREAKING IN STONE PRODUCTS IN THE HOME

Like Mother Nature herself, natural stone is both rugged and vulnerable. Each stone requires specific care and maintenance, and homeowners often experience a period of adjustment as they become accustomed to the requirements of caring for their floors or countertops.

Ask an expert about the different requirements and characteristics. Soapstone, for example, is a beautiful, soft stone with an antique patina many people love. Accumulated stains and scratches just add to the look. Granite, on the other hand, will not stain.

A professional can educate you about the specific characteristics of each stone product so you make an informed decision on what products will best serve the lifestyle of your family.

CHOOSING STONE – A UNIQUE EXPERIENCE

Once a decision to use a natural stone is made, begin your search right away. By allowing plenty of time to discover the full realm of choices, you'll be able to choose a stone and finish that brings luster and value to your home, without the pressure of a deadline. If you order imported stone, it can take months for delivery. Be prepared to visit your supplier's warehouse to inspect the stone that will be used in your home. Natural stone varies – piece to piece, box to box – a slab can vary in color from one end to the other. If you understand this degree of unpredictable irregularity is unavoidable, it will help you approach the selection in a realistic way.

STRONG AND ELEGANT COUNTERTOPS

The quest for quality and style does not stop until the countertops are selected. Today's countertop marketplace is brimming with man-made products that add high style without sacrificing strength and resiliency.

As the functions of kitchens become broader, the demand for aesthetics continues to increase dramatically. For lasting beauty with incredible design sensibilities, manmade solid surfaces are a very popular choice. The overwhelming number of possibilities and combinations in selecting countertops makes it vital to work with specialists who are quality-oriented. Countertops represent a significant investment in a custom home, and quality, performance and style must be the primary considerations in any decision. Established professionals, like those introduced in your Home Book, have a reputation for expert installation and service of the top quality products that define luxury.

MAKE COUNTERTOP CHOICES EARLY

Since decisions on cabinetry are often made far in advance, it's best to make a countertop choice concurrently.

Expect to spend at least two weeks visiting showrooms and acquainting yourself with design and materials. Take along paint chips, samples of cabinet and flooring materials, and any pictures of the look you're trying to achieve. Expect a solid surface custom counter order to take at least five weeks to arrive.

AN ARRAY OF COUNTERTOP CHOICES

You'll face a field of hundreds of colors and textures of solid surfacing, laminates, ceramic tile, natural stone, wood and stainless or enameled steel. Poured concrete counters also are finding their way into luxury kitchens in the area.

Laminate or color-through laminate offer hundreds of colors, patterns and textures, many of which convincingly mimic the look of solid surfacing or granite. Enjoying growing popularity in countertop application, are the natural stones, those staggeringly gorgeous slabs of granite, marble or slate, which offer the timeless look of quality and luxury. Naturally quarried stone is extremely durable and brings a dramatic beauty and texture to the kitchen or bath. For endless color and pattern possibilities, ceramic tile is a highly durable option. Manmade resin-based solid surfacing materials offer many of the same benefits as stone. These surfaces are fabricated for durability and beauty, and new choices offer a visual depth that is astounding to the eye. It can be bent, carved, or sculpted. Elaborate edges can be cut into a solid surface counter and sections can be carved out to accommodate other surface materials, such as stainless steel or marble. Best known for superior durability, solid surfaces stand up to scratches, heat and water.

FINDING THE BEST SOURCE FOR MATERIALS

If you're building or remodeling your home, your designer, builder or architect will help you develop some ideas and find a supplier for the material you choose. Reputable suppliers, like those featured in the Home Book, are experienced in selecting the best products and providing expert installation. Go visit a showroom or office – their knowledge will be invaluable to you. The intricacies and idiosyncrasies of natural products, and the sheer volume of possibilities in fabricated surfaces, can be confounding on your own. ∎

BE CREATIVE!

Mix and match counter top materials for optimum functionality and up-to-date style. Install a butcher block for chopping vegetables and slicing breads, a slab of marble for rolling pastry and bakery dough, granite on an island for overall elegance, and solid surfaces for beauty and durability around the sinks and cooktop areas.

215

MAKE IT CONCRETE

This material is a versatile and indestructible choice, available in a variety of colors and textures. Sealed concrete can be made with creative borders, scored, sandblasted or stained. A strong, natural material, it can be made to look like other materials and natural stone.

Ceramic Tile

J & L TILE CREATIONS..**(281) 701-2119**
2842 Pepperwood, Sugar Land   Fax:(281) 277-7958
See ad on page 217
<u>e-mail:</u> johnhitzel@aol.com

Floor Coverings

VENETIAN BLIND & FLOOR CARPET ONE ....**(713) 528-2404**
2504 Bissonnet, Houston   Fax:(713) 528-0327
See ad on page 208D
<u>Website:</u> www.vbaf.com
<u>e-mail:</u> david.bellamy@vbaf.com

Flooring & Countertops

216

EXOTIC FLOORING..**(713) 785-9117**
3301 Fondren, Ste. B, Houston   Fax:(713) 785-5480
See ad on page 219

FLOOR DESIGNERS..**(281) 679-5577**
2703 Hwy 6 S., Ste. 300, Houston   Fax:(281) 679-5815
See ad on page 208B, 208C
Website: www.floordesignershoustontexas.com
e-mail: adjamal2002@yahoo.com

Houston's Premier
Home & Design
Sourcebook

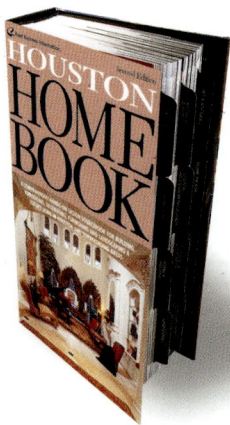

The **Houston Home Book** is your final destination when searching for home remodeling, building and decorating resources. This comprehensive, hands-on sourcebook to building, remodeling, decorating, furnishing and landscaping a luxury home is required reading for the serious and discriminating homeowner. With more than 300 full-color, beautiful pages, the **Houston Home Book** is the most complete and well-organized reference to the home industry. This hardcover volume covers all aspects of the process, includes listings of hundreds of industry professionals, and is accompanied by informative and valuable editorial discussing the most recent trends. Ordering your copy of the **Houston Home Book** now can ensure that you have the blueprints to your dream home, in your hand, today.

Visit our online store at
www.theashleygroup.com

O R D E R   F O R M

THE HOUSTON HOME BOOK

☐ YES, please send me _____ copies of the HOUSTON HOME BOOK at $39.95 per book, plus $4 Shipping & Handling per book.

Total amount enclosed: $_____ Please charge my: ☐ VISA   ☐ MasterCard   ☐ American Express

Card # _____ Exp. Date _____

Signature _____

Name _____ Phone (_____) _____

Address _____ E-mail _____

City _____ State _____ Zip Code _____

Send order to: Attn: Book Sales — Marketing, The Ashley Group — Reed Business Information 2000 Clearwater Drive, Oak Brook, IL 60523
Or Call Toll Free: 888.458.1750 Fax: 630.288.7949 E-mail ashleybooksales@reedbusiness.com

All orders must be accompanied by check, money order or credit card # for full amount. All book orders are nonrefundable.

EXOTIC FLOORING
"QUALITY IS EXCELLENCE"
SHOWROOM AVAILABLE

We are your "One Stop Shop" for all your stone needs
• Marble • Granite • Limestone • Slate • Tile • Slab •
• Tile Fireplace Mantels • Staircases • Granite Countertops •
• Tile Foundations • Furniture Tops •

Fabricators • Installers • Retail • Wholesale

3301 Fondren Ste. B   Houston, TX 77063
713-785-9117   713-785-5480

FLOORING & COUNTERTOPS

Berber carpet
A flecked carpet available in looped, cut pile or frieze styles. The term "Berber" is generally attached to looped styles of carpet that were reintroduced in the early 1980's.

Black galaxy
Deep black granite commonly used for kitchen and bath surfaces.

Distressed flooring
Hardwood floor that has become colored and altered with age and wear. This process is also artificially duplicated to achieve an antique appearance in new flooring.

Floating wood floor
A floor in which the panels are completely separated from the structural floor or foundation by means of an underlayment or mounting devices.

Shivakashi
Summer yellow to ivory and brown colored granite from India, popular for countertops and backsplashes.

Sodalite
Striking blue and white marble often used in tiles, counters, bathtubs and backsplashes.

Soapstone
Massive soft stone that contains a high proportion of talc; frequently used for kitchen surfaces and hand-carved ornaments.

Special Matrix Terrazzo
Flooring consisting of colored aggregate and organic matrix.

Stained Concrete
Concrete stained using a hydrochloric acid wash that gives it a color and finish that can be altered to mimic natural stone or other surface effects.

Stamped Concrete
A process whereby a pattern is set into wet concrete that can imitate, for example, a stone or brick pattern. Various systems and tools can be used to create a wide variety of appearances.

Tongue & groove
Boards or lumber that has been planed smooth and cut so that a tongue along one edge of a board fits into a groove on an adjacent piece.

White Oak
A hard, heavy, durable wood, gray to reddish brown in color; especially used for flooring, paneling and trim.

Wilton Carpet
A velvet cut-pile carpet, woven with loops on a Jacquard loom, usually having excellent wearing qualities.

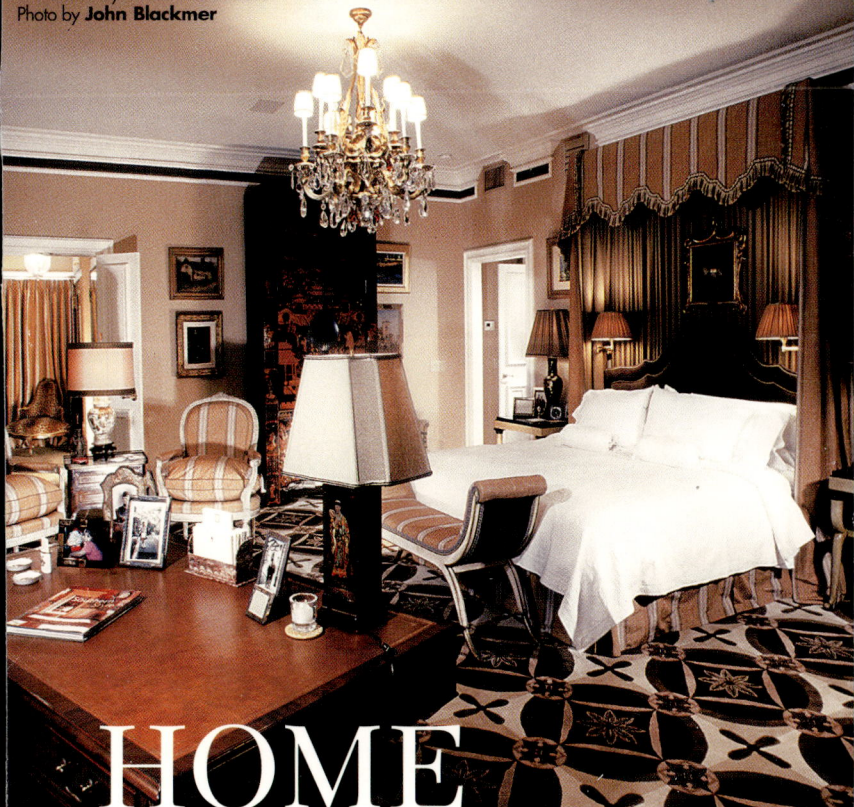

HOME
FURNISHINGS
&
DECORATING

Family owned and operated since 1969,
Alyson Jon Interiors is a Houston Landmark.
From classic to contemporary, we offer
our clients the most incredible selection of
furnishings and accessories in the city.
We also offer full scale interior design services
to help you create a special look for one room
or a custom plan for your entire home.

TAKE TIME TO CHOOSE FURNITURE

FOCUS

Is there an architectural focus point in the room, a fireplace, a skylight or brilliant picture window? If not, consider creating focus with a significant piece of furniture, possibly custom designed, like an elaborate entertainment center in the family room or an elegant headboard in the master bedroom.

ACHIEVING A BALANCE

For a calming, soothing home, consider designing your rooms around the ancient Chinese study of Feng Shui. Not a religion, the science of Feng Shui is used to organize furnishings and decorative accessories in a natural way to balance the energy of the home and create a harmonious environment. Indoor water features, strategic placement of mirrors and open vessels, along with careful consideration of the arrangement of furniture in each room are all part of designing a Feng Shui environment.

You'll be living with your choices for many years to come, so take your time. Try to define why you like what you like. Look through shelter magazines, visit decorator homes and furniture showrooms. When you see a piece or arrangement you like, try analyze what you like about it. Is it the color, the sty of the piece, the texture of the fabric? Recognizing common elements you are drawn to will help you hone and refine your personal style.

As you start out, be sure to ruthlessly assess your current interior. Clear out pieces that need to b replaced or no longer work with your lifestyle, even you have no clear idea of what you'll be replacing them with. Sometimes empty space makes visualizin something new much easier.

When furnishing a new room, consider creating a focus by concentrating on an architectural element or selecting one important piece, like a Chinese Chippendale-style daybed or an original Arts & Crafts spindle table. Or, make your focus a special piece you already own.

To make the most of your time when visiting showrooms, take along your blueprint or a detailed drawing with measurements, door and window placements, and special architectural features. If your spouse or anyone else will be involved in the final decision, try to shop together to eliminate return trips. The majority of stores can deliver most furniture within eight weeks, but special custom pieces may take up to 16 weeks.

Be open-minded and accept direction. Rely on your interior designer or a qualified store designer to help direct your search and keep you within the scale of your floor plan. Salespeople at top stores can help you find exactly what you're seeking, and, if you ask them, guide you away from inappropriate decisions toward more suitable alternatives. Their firsthand knowledge of pricing, products and features is invaluable when it comes to finding the best quality for your money.

As you seek these tangible expressions of your personal style, keep these thoughts in mind:

• What are your priorities? Develop a list of "must have," "want to have," and "dreaming about."

• What major pieces will be with you for a long time? Allow a lion's share of your budget for these.

• What colors or styles are already established through the flooring, walls, windows, or cabinetry? Keep swatches with you, if possible.

• Does the piece reflect your tastes? Don't be influenced too strongly by what looks great in a showroom or designer house.

221

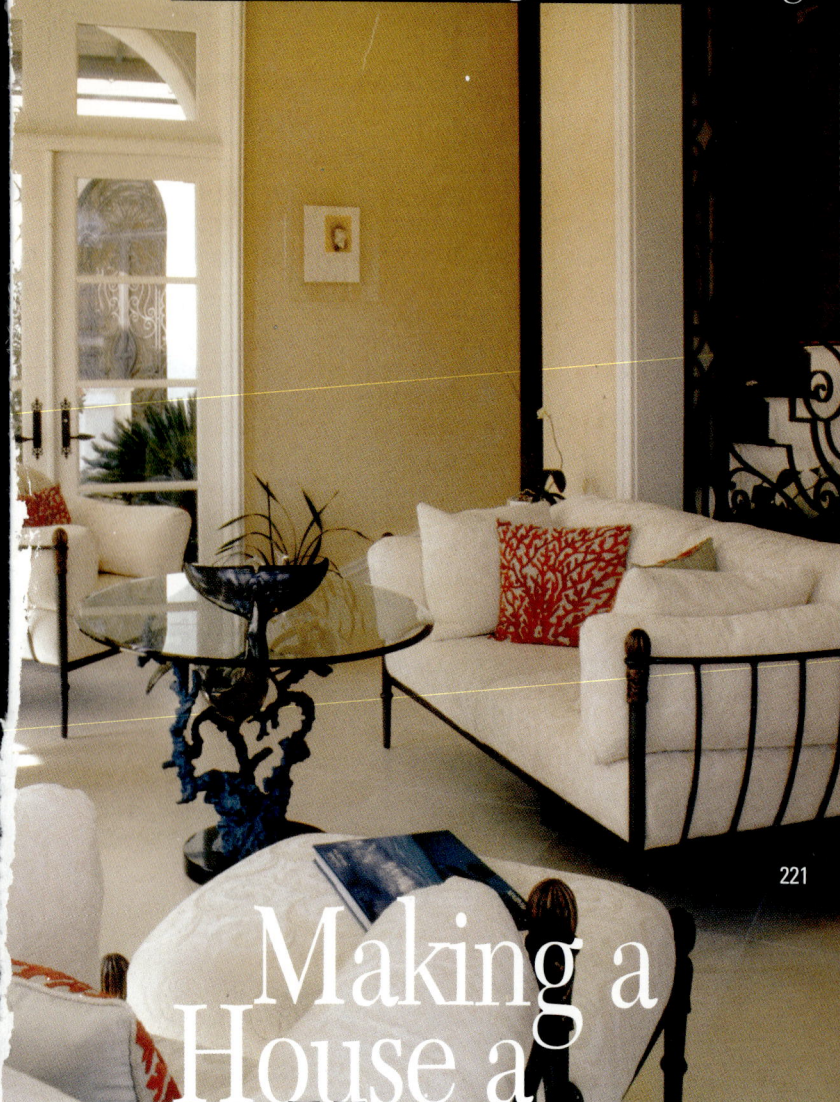

Making a House a Home

Everyone wants to put their personal touch on their home, and the surest way to do that is to select the home furnishings that reflect your personality and lifestyle. Is Venetian plaster your thing? Do you enjoy the charm and warmth of a country home? Perhaps you envision yourself as someone on the cutting-edge, and you lean toward contemporary décor. Acquiring the right furniture, window and wall treatments will make your house sing your own personal song.

Photo courtesy of **The Bryan Design Associates**

• Does the piece fit the overall decorating scheme? Although the days of strict adherence to one style per room are over, it's still necessary to use coordinated styles.

• Is the piece comfortable? Before you buy, sit on the chair, recline on the sofa, pull a chair up to the table.

• Can you get the furnishings through the doorway, up the elevator, or down the stairs?

• Will a piece work for your family's lifestyle? Choose upholstery fabrics, colors and fixtures that will enhance, not hinder, your everyday life.

DESIGNED FOR YOU

The ultimate in expression of personal style, a piece of custom designed furniture is akin to functional art for your home. A custom furniture designer can create virtually any piece you need to fill a special space in your home and satisfy your desire for owning a unique one-of-a-kind.

Some of the most talented, best known designers working in this area today are listed in the following pages of the Home Book. You can contact them directly, or through your interior designer. At an initial meeting you'll see examples of the designer's work and answer questions like:

• What kind of piece do you want? Freestanding entertainment system, dining table, armoire?

• What functions must it serve? It is a piece of art, but the furniture still must function in ways that make it practical and usable. Explain your needs clearly.

• Do you have favorite woods, materials or colors? As with ordering custom woodwork, the possibilities are almost unlimited. Different woods can be painted or finished differently for all kinds of looks. It's best to have some ideas in mind.

• Are you open to new ideas and approaches? If you'd like the designer to suggest new ways of reaching your goal, let him or her know.

Seek out a furniture designer whose portfolio excites you, who you can communicate with, and who you trust to deliver your project in a top quality, professional manner. Ask for a couple of design options for your piece. Make sure you and the designer are in agreement regarding finishes, materials, stain or paint samples you want to see, and a completion date. Most charge a 50 percent deposit at the beginning with the balance due upon completion. If you decide not to go ahead with construction of a piece, expect to be billed a designer's fee. A commissioned piece of furniture

FROM THE FLOOR UP

Your carpets, rugs or flooring set the stage for your design. Whether a simple backdrop or the starring role, it's important to determine which part you want your floor treatments to take at the outset of your decorating project.

'FAUX' FINISH TROMPE L'OEIL?

223

Any painting technique replicating another look is called a 'faux' (false) finish. There are many methods to achieve wonderful individual effects. Trompe l'oeil (fool the eye) is a mural painting that creates illusion through perspective. A wall becomes an arched entry to a garden.

requires a reasonable amount of time to get from start to finish. If you want an entertainment system for Super Bowl Sunday, make your final design decisions when you take down the Halloween decorations. Keep in mind that the process cannot be rushed.

ILLUMINATING IDEAS

Lighting can be the focal point of a room, or it can be so subtle that it's almost invisible. The trick is knowing what you want to accomplish. Indeed, when we remember a place as cozy and elegant, or cold and uncomfortable, we're feeling the emotional power of illumination.

The industry is filled with options and combinations, from fixtures and bulbs to dimmers and integrated systems. Top lighting retailers in the area employ in-house design consultants to guide you, or you can employ a residential lighting designer.

To deliver a superior lighting scheme, a designer must know:

• What are your needs? Lighting falls into three categories – general, task, and atmospheric. A study/work area, a cozy nook or a kitchen each require different lighting.

• What feeling are you trying to create?

• What "givens" are you working with? Where are your windows or skylights? The use of artificial, indoor light depends to a great degree on the natural light coming in.

• What materials are on the floor and what colors are on the walls and ceiling? This affects how well your lighting will reflect, or "bounce."

• Where is your furniture placed, and how big are individual pieces? This is especially important when you're choosing a dining room chandelier.

• If you're replacing lighting, why are you replacing it? Know the wattage, for instance, if a current light source is no longer bright enough.

• Are there energy/environmental concerns? Lighting consumes 12 to 15 percent of the electricity used in the home. An expert can develop a plan that maximizes energy efficiency.

WINDOW DRESSING

The well-appointed room includes window treatments in keeping with the style of the home and furnishings. Yet it's also important to consider how your window treatments will need to function in your setting. Will they be required to control light,

WHAT'S YOUR STYLE?

Consider these characteristics of different styles: Formal-Dark, polished woods; smooth, tightly woven fabrics; symmetrically placed furnishings. **Casual**-Lighter woods; textured, loosely woven fabrics, asymmetric placement. **Contemporary**-Artistic, sculptural furnishings with smooth, clean lines; bold splashes of color and carefully placed artwork. **French Country**-Aged, carved wood furnishings; textiles feature earth-tones mixed with intense colors; accessorized with wrought iron, pottery and baskets. **Rustic**-Sturdy, extremely textural furnishings of polished logs, softened with cushions and pillows in colorful fabrics. **Shabby Chic**-White furniture and accents, slipcovers, overstuffed upholstery and "old" looking accessories. **Tuscan**-Sturdy heavily distressed wood furnishings with terra cotta tile, stone or marble accents; bright fabrics; washed or faux-finished painted surfaces.

224

or provide privacy as well? Some windows in your home may need just a top treatment as a finishing touch, while a soaring window wall might require sun-blocking draperies or blinds to minimize heat build-up or ultraviolet damage.

How window treatments will be installed is another design question to consider – inside or outside the window frame, from the top of the window to the sill or from ceiling to floor? Take these points into consideration when designing your window treatments:

• How much privacy do you require? If you love the look of light and airy sheers, remember they become transparent at night and you may need blinds or shades as well.

• Is light control necessary? This is usually a must for bedroom window treatments, as well as for windows with southern or western exposures

• Do you want to take advantage of a beautiful view of the landscape or hide an unsightly view of the building next door?

• Are there any structural elements such as built-in cabinets, outlets or vents near the window to consider?

• Are your windows a focal point of the room or the background that puts the finishing touch on your room design?

• What role will the choice of fabric play? The fabric can unify the whole, standout as the focus, or add another note to the rhythm of the room.

PAINTING OUTSIDE THE FRAMES

Through their travels, reading and exposure to art and design, sophisticated homeowners are aware of the beauty that can be added to their homes with specialty decorative painting. They see perfect canvases for unique works of art in walls, furniture and fabrics. The demand for beautiful art applied directly to walls, stairs or furniture has created a renaissance in decorative painting. Faux finishes, trompe l'oeil and murals have joined the traditional finishes of paint, wallpaper and stain for consideration in outstanding residential interiors.

Specialty painters can help you fine-tune your idea, or develop a concept from scratch. At your initial meeting, discuss your ideas, whether they're crystal clear or barely there. Don't be apprehensive if you don't have a clear idea. Artists are by profession visually creative, and by asking questions and sharing ideas, you can develop a concept together.

Ask to see samples of his or her other work, and if possible, visit homes or buildings where the work has been done. Ask for, and call, references. Find out

CUSTOM DESIGNING A CHERRY WOOD TABLE

What might it actually cost to have a custom designed piece of furniture made for you?
Here is a general estimate of the costs involved in the custom design and construction of a 48 in. x 96 in. dining room table.
• **Trees harvested (felled) ($30/hr x 2 hours):**
   $60
• **Trees sawn and dried:**
   $175
• **Design (included in the project cost)**
• **Labor cost (fine sanding, construction, varnishing):**
   $5,000
• **Special materials (included in cost)**

   Total:
   $5,235

RECLAIMING CHARACTER

Magnificently unique custom-designed furnishings can be made of wood reclaimed from building renovations or demolitions. Another option is to use new wood, hand-distressed to lend it the character of an older piece.

if the work was completed on time and on budget. Based on your initial conversations, a painter can give you a rough estimate based on the size of the room and the finish you've discussed. You can expect the artist to get back to you with sample drawings, showing color and technique, usually within a week.

Surface preparation, such as stripping and patching, is not usually done by the specialty painter. Ask for recommendations of professionals to do this work if you don't have a painter you already use.

THE GREAT OUTDOORS

As homeowners strive to expand comfortable living space into their yards, top quality outdoor furniture manufacturers respond with new and innovative styles. Before you shop for outdoor furniture, think about:

• What look do you like? The intricate patterns of wrought iron? The smooth and timeless beauty of silvery teak wood? The sleek design of sturdy aluminum?

• What pieces do you need? Furnishing larger decks and terraces requires careful planning.

• Will you store the furniture in the winter or will it stay outdoors under cover?

• Can you see the furniture from inside the house? Make sure the outdoor furnishings won't distract from the established inside or outside design.

TICKLING THE IVORIES

A new or professionally reconditioned piano makes an excellent contribution to the elegance and lifestyle of a growing number of area homes. Pianos add a dimension of personality that no ordinary piece of furniture can match. They are recognized for their beauty, visually and acoustically.

First time piano buyers may be astonished at the range of choices they have and the variables that will influence their eventual decision. Go to the showrooms that carry the best brand name pianos. Not only will you be offered superior quality instruments, but you'll also get the benefit of the sales staff's professional knowledge and experience. Questions that you need to answer will include:

• Who are the primary players of the instrument?

• What level of players are they (serious, beginners)?

• Who are their teachers?

• What is the size of the room the piano will be placed in?

THE PRICE OF GETTING ORGANIZED

• An 8 ft. closet, round steel chrome plated rods, double and single hang, with a five-drawer unit: $800 to $1,000
• His-and-Hers walk-in closet, full length and double hang rods, two five-drawer units, foldable storage space, mirrored back wall, shoe rack: $1,000 to $4,000
• Conversion of a full-size bedroom into closet area with islands, custom designed cabinets with full extension drawers and decorative hardware, mirrors, jewelry drawers, and many other luxury appointments: $15,000
• Customized desk area, with file drawers, computer stand and slide shelves for printer, keyboard and mouse pad, high pressure surface on melamine with shelves above desk: $3,000
• Average garage remodel, with open and closed storage, sports racks for bikes and fishing poles, a small workbench, and a 4 ft. x 8 ft. pegboard, installed horizontally: $2,500

• What are your preferences in wood color or leg shape?

• Are you interested in software packages that convert your instrument into a player piano?

Pianos represent a significant financial investment, one that will not depreciate, and may actually appreciate over time. If a new piano is out of your financial range, ask about the store's selection of reconditioned instruments that they've acquired through trades. The best stores recondition these pieces to a uniformly high standard of excellence and are good options for you to consider. These stores also hold occasional promotions, when special pricing will be in effect for a period of time.

THE HOME OFFICE COMES INTO ITS OWN

The home office has become a "must have" room for many homeowners. More businesses are being operated from home, and increasing numbers of companies are allowing, even encouraging, telecommuting. Spreading out on the dining room table or kitchen table is no longer an efficient option.

Because the home office often requires specific wiring and lighting, be sure your architect, designer and builder are involved in the planning process. If you're simply outfitting an existing room to be your home office, designers on staff at fine furniture stores can guide you. However, it's still most practical to get some architectural input for optimum comfort and functionality of the space.

While some aspects of home furnishings may be easy to overlook, such as storage and lighting, you should give great attention to all of them. The construction of your dream home will give you a place to live, but the way it is furnished will let you live in the style you want. ■

PROJECT FILE

A project file with carpet, fabric, wallpaper and paint samples, floor plans, a tape measure, a calendar, and a phone list of everyone working on your project can really enhance your decorating experience. With your file in hand, decisions can be made on the spot without having to check if the piece matches or fits into your overall plan.

Accessories

PLANTS N PETALS ....**(713) 840-9191**
3810 Westheimer, Houston   Fax:(713) 840-8830
See ad on page 233
<u>Website:</u> www.plantsnpetals.net
<u>e-mail:</u> info@plantsnpetals.net

SOMETHING SPECIAL ....**(832) 249-8607**
12703-A Cutten Rd, Houston   Fax:(832) 249-8306
See ad on page 231

Closet &
Garage Systems

CLOSET FACTORY ....**(281) 355-7676**
2530 Old Louetta Loop, Suite 128, Spring   Fax:(281) 288-0200
See ad on page 237
<u>Website:</u> www.closetfactory.com
<u>e-mail:</u> closet@wt.net

Furniture

ALYSON JON INTERIORS ....**(713) 524-3171**
2401 Bissonnet Street, Houston   Fax:(713) 524-2514
See ad on page 220B, 220C
<u>Website:</u> www.alysonjon.com

Home
Furnishings

ACCENTS FINE FURNITURE ....**(713) 541-3555**
7075 Southwest Freeway, Houston   Fax:(713) 541-4888
See ad on page 229
<u>e-mail:</u> accentsfurniture@sbcglobal.net

PLUS KLASSE, INC....**(713) 626-4249**
7026 Old Katy Road, Suite 250, Houston   Fax:(713) 626-3938
See ad on page 230
<u>Website:</u> www.plusklasse.com
<u>e-mail:</u> info@plusklasse.com

continued on page **232**

Accents
Fine Furniture & Accessories

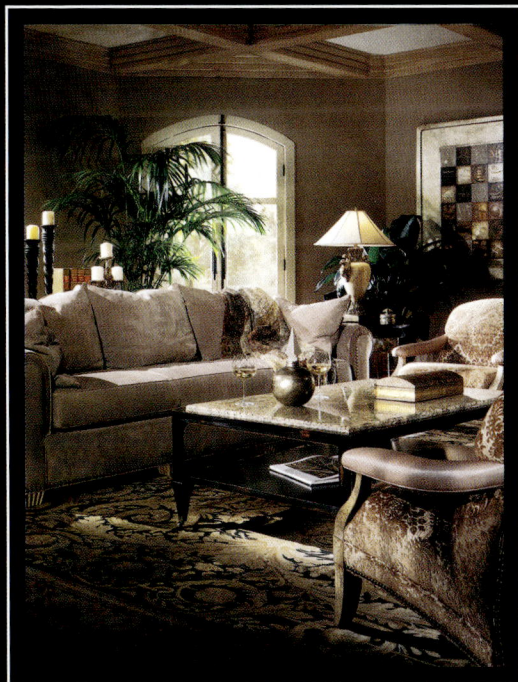

2950 Fondren
Houston, TX 77063
Tel: 713-785-3702
Fax: 713-785-3707

7075 SW Freeway
Houston, TX 77074
Tel: 713-541-3555
Fax: 713-541-4888

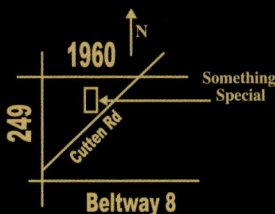

continued from page 228

Lighting

HOUSE OF GLASS ....**(713) 528-5289**
3319 Louisiana, Houston   Fax:(713) 528-2562
See ad on page 235
<u>e-mail:</u> houseofglass@excite.com

LIGHT SOURCE ....**(281) 496-5454**
14900 Westheimer, Houston   Fax:(281) 496-3933
See ad on page 234
<u>Website:</u> www.builders-lighting-hardware.com
<u>e-mail:</u> info@oldjack.com

Specialty
Wall Finishes

MISHA CREATIONS...**(281) 650-0500**
See ad on page 220D
<u>Website:</u> www.mishacreations.com
<u>e-mail:</u> mishacreations@sbcglobal.net

Window
Tinting

SUNSET GLASS TINTING ....**(713) 777-3355**
12847 Capricorn, Stafford   Fax:(713) 777-0045
See ad on page 236
<u>Website:</u> www.sunsetglasstinting.com
<u>e-mail:</u> sunset1@pdq.net

232

LIGHT SOURCE

**14900 Westheimer Rd
Houston, Texas 77082
281-496-5454**

QUOIZEL®

OLD JACKSONVILLE

HOUSE of GLASS

Houston's Oldest Fine Lighting Showroom

Original Owners since 1948

Premier source for antique and reproduction chandeliers, sconces, and mirrors. Our company also carries home accessories, specialty fireplace accessories and an outstanding line of outside gas lights. House of Glass services include Restoration of Chandeliers, Sconce and Candelabras.

3319 Louisiana Street, Houston, Texas 77006
713.528.5289

VISTA®
WINDOW FILM

SUNSET
GLASS TINTING

Protect Your Home's Interior From the
Harmful Effects of the Sun.

Serving Houston Since 1988

713.777.3355
www.sunsetglasstinting.com

ASID
Industry Partner

BBB

YOU'LL STILL HAVE NOTHING TO WEAR.
BUT AT LEAST YOU'LL KNOW FOR SURE.

Our expert Designers can create a custom closet that's stylish, efficient and built around you. You'll know exactly what you have, and exactly where it is. And if you still can't find the perfect outfit, it's a good excuse to go shopping.

FREE INSTALLATION

closet f actory

800.430.2999   281.355.7676
Call for a free design consultation
www.closetfactory.com

HOME FURNISHINGS

Armoire
A large, often ornate, cabinet or wardrobe.

Bare bottom chair
A northeastern American concept in which a chair has no finish applied to the bottom of the seat so that, on a special occasion, such as a wedding, friends and family may express their feelings of admiration, appreciation, or future well wishes in writing on the bottom of the seat.

Biedermeier
Of or relating to a type of furniture developed in Germany during the first half of the 19th century and modeled after French Empire styles. It is essentially Empire furniture shorn of its ormolu mounts, excessive gilding and aggressive self-importance. Its original geometric shape often leads it to being described as the forerunner of modern furniture.

Contemporary
Furnishings of this sort are characteristic of the present (or modern) trends in design, generally an innovative form or style of creation that emerged after 1960.

Patina
Visible natural age and wear on a piece of furniture created by a couple of decades worth of frequent use and care. The most common versions are thin oxide films on old metals (copper and bronze develop a green film) or the soft wear marks and bare edges that occur in painted or stained wood. This effect can also be artificially induced or imitated through various methods of faux finishing.

Plantation shutters
Interior, louvered shutters made from hardwood and designed to control light, ventilation and privacy. Generally covering the entire expanse of the window or doorway when in use.

Queen Anne furnishings
Queen Anne (England, 1702 to 1714) has her name attributed to the popular furniture style even though it did not appear until 1720, nearly a decade after her death. Often referred to as the Age of Walnut, most of this furniture of this time period was produced from the deep walnut stock, and was popular for its aesthetically pleasing S-curves that start at the legs and move up through the piece. The wood was mostly plain with the exception of eye-catching carvings on legs, chair backs, drawers and the top of cabinets. The Queen Anne style is the most reproduced of all American furniture.

Soft furnishings
Decorating elements ranging from valences, draperies, curtains and other window treatments to cushions, pillows, bedding and throws.

Venetian window
A window of large size, characteristic of Neoclassical styles, divided by columns or piers resembling pilasters, into three lights, the middle one of which is usually wider than the others, and is sometimes arched.

ART&
ANTIQUES

Carl Moore

❖ **Monday – Friday** 9:30 – 5:30
❖ **Thursday** 9:30 – 7:00
❖ **Saturday** 10:00 – 5:00

www.carlmooreantiques.net

1610 Bissonnet ❖ Houston, TX 77005 USA

Telephone 713-524-2502 ❖ Facsimile 713-524-2535

ALLART
Museum Quality Framing

Allart Director
Rose Avera

Allart
2635 Revere
Houston, TX 77098
713-526-3631

Allart Gallery's inspired design, exquisite craftsmanship and outstanding custom framing has been serving the Houston community since 1954.

Stocking one of the largest inventories of 22kt gold and custom reproduction antique moldings and hand colored French mats, Allart's professional staff specializes in creating and executing the the prefect design for your art and memorabilia .

Offering the finest quality materials and craftsmanship with every endeavor, Allart's superior personalized service guarantees lasting pleasure and the integrity of your fine art.

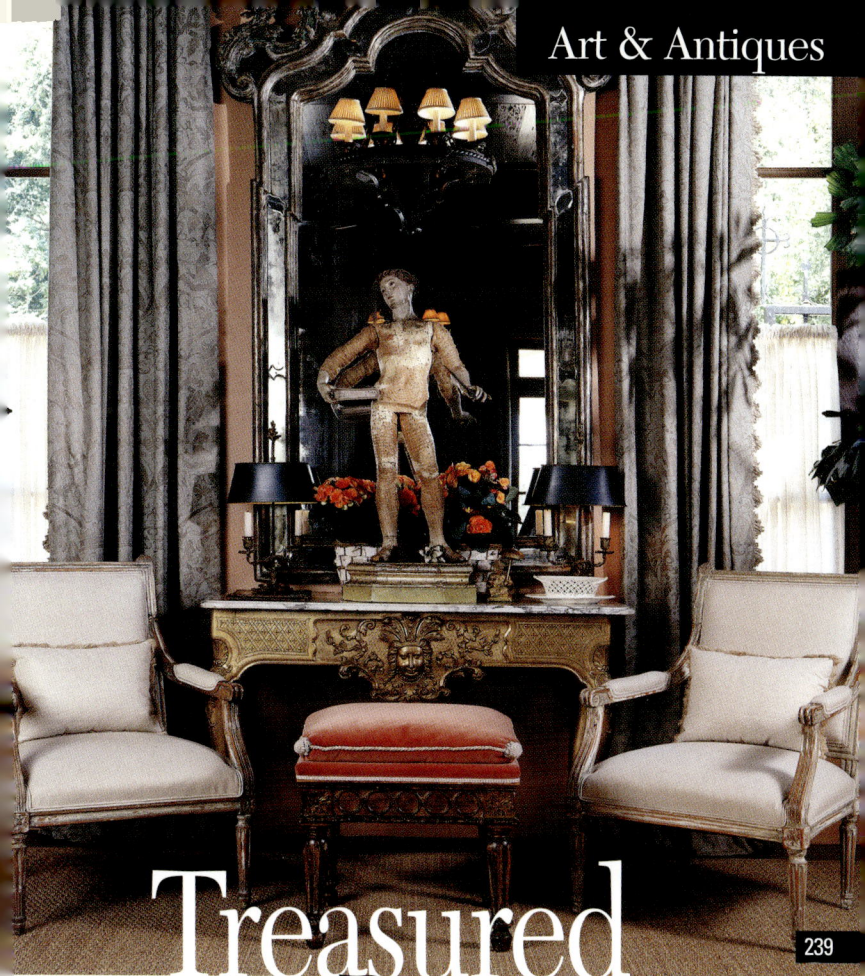

239

Treasured Pieces

"All art," said Oscar Wilde, "is quite useless." On some level, that may be true, since a painting won't keep you warm at night, nor will a priceless antique feed you. But that painting or antique can speak to us as no other "functional" objects in our homes can. We can be comforted, delighted, or transported to another place by a work of art or prized antique.

A part of an owner's soul is reflected in every piece of art he or she chooses to display in their home. Art and antiques speak to their owners and anyone who passes by, offering the latter a glimpse of the homeowner's personality. A piece of art can take someone to a place he's never been or one he's long left behind. An antique can provide a real connection to one's ancestors. Art and antiques can infuse a home with the character and personality of its owner, telling a story along the way. For anyone wishing to make their house truly home, art is quite useful indeed.

Photo courtesy of **Roland Bishop Photography**

A PIECE OF THE PAST

Part of the pleasure of collecting art or antiques is learning about them. Many homeowners buy a particular painting or sculpture they love, and find that following the art form or the artists becomes a lifetime passion.

The best place to start to familiarize yourself with art is at one of the many wonderful museums in your area. Wander through historic homes in the different historic neighborhoods of the city and get an idea of what the art feels like in a home environment. Go to auctions. Buy the catalog and attend the viewing. At the sale, you'll begin to get an idea of the values of different types of items. Finally, get to know a dealer. Most are pleased to help you learn and want to see more people develop a lifetime love affair with art, similar to their own. If a dealer seems too busy or isn't genuinely interested in helping you, then go to another dealer.

Haunt the local bookstores and newsstands. There are many publications dedicated to these fields.

Homeowners find their way to a love of antiques by many different paths. Some are adding to an inherited collection that connects them with past generations of family or with the location of their birth. Some are passionate about pottery or porcelain, clocks or dolls, and want to expand their knowledge while building a lifetime collection.

Antique furniture, artwork and collectibles also can be used to make a singular statement in an interior. Through a 19th Century English chest, an American Arts & Crafts table, or a beloved collection of Tiffany glass vases, homeowners put a personal signature on their interior design.

Making the right selection is as much a matter of knowledge and experience as it is taste and personal aesthetic. As top quality antique paintings, photographs and other desirable items become more difficult to find, getting expert guidance in identifying good and worthwhile investments is crucial. An interior designer or the knowledgeable professionals at the top galleries in the area can help you determine the value of pieces you are considering by assessing these four characteristics:

• Rarity – In general, the more difficult it is to find similar pieces, the greater the value. Try to determine how many comparable pieces exist. However, it is possible to be too rare. If there are too few similar pieces in circulation, there may be limited demand.

• Quality – The quality of the original materials and workmanship affects the value significantly.

• Provenance – The history of a piece, how many owners it has had, is its provenance. A piece with only a few owners has a better provenance.

• Condition – The more that remains of the original finish, the more valuable the piece. However, in some cases, small imperfections can help to establish authenticity.

When you visit an antique store or gallery, be prepared to seriously consider what type of investment you wish to make and how it will work in a given interior.

If you are pursuing pieces to add to an existing collection, do your research to determine which dealers and galleries in the area cater to your interests. Or, check with a favorite gallery for information. Be open to ideas and suggestions, especially when you're just beginning a collection, or a search for a special antique. There is so much to know about so many different objects, time periods, and design, that it truly does take a lifetime to develop an expertise.

VISITING ART GALLERIES

More than anything else, choosing to make beautiful, distinctive art objects a part of your home brings the joy of living with beautiful things into the daily life of yourself, your family and your guests.

The most important rule to know as your begin or continue to add art to your home is that there truly are no "rights or wrongs." Find what reaches you on an emotional level, and then begin to learn about it.

Use your eyes and react with your heart. Look at art magazines and books. Visit the museums in town, and those in other cities as you travel. Go to the galleries. Visit many of them for the widest exposure to different possibilities. Use the Internet to visit gallery and museum sites from all over the world. Let only your sense of beauty and aesthetics guide you at this point. Consider other constraints after you've identified the objects of your desire.

EXPERT ADVICE

The most reputable art gallery owners and dealers have earned their reputation by establishing an expertise in their field, and serving their clients well.

Buying from these established, respected professionals offers many benefits. Their considerable knowledge of and exposure to art translates into opinions that mean a great deal. You can trust the advice and education they offer you. They've done considerable research and evaluation before any item gets placed in their gallery, and determined that it's a good quality item, both in terms of artistic merit and market value. You can also rest assured that they will stand behind the authenticity of what they present in their galleries. Most offer free consultations, trade-back arrangements, and installation, and will help you with selling your art at some point in the future as your collection grows, you change residences, or your tastes change.

VALUE JUDGMENTS

Buy for love, not money. This is the advice we heard time and again from the best art galleries. Not all art appreciates financially – often it fluctuates over the years according to the artist's career, consumer tastes, and the state of the overall economy. If you love what you own and have been advised well by a knowledgeable professional, you'll be happiest with your investment.

TARNISH OR PATINA?

If your collection includes decorative metal objects like an engraved silver platter or brass handles on an antique chest, tarnish may become an issue. In some cases, the tarnish, caused by oxidation, can add subtle shadings and a beautiful patina to the piece. Before you polish, decide if the piece is more authentic with the tarnish. If so, relax and enjoy.

241

MAKE AN APPOINTMENT

When you have identified a gallery or dealer you admire, call for an appointment to discuss your needs. Most professionals appreciate knowing you will be visiting at a specific time so they can have additional help on hand to attend to other customers.

THE FINESSE OF FINE ART

You know what you like, but how much might it actually cost to fill your home with art? Following is one example, for the analysis, research and procurement of six art pieces.

Before the project begins, a budget is established based on the type of art desired (sculpture, drawings, paintings, tapestry), the quality of the art, scale, and provenance.

**The art:
A print for the hallway;
a 4-ft. tall classical bronze sculpture;
a still-life painting;
two tapestries;
a Dufy painting;
Total: $55,000**

**Additional expenses:
Appraisal services;
framing;
insurance;
consultation fees;
security;
Total; $19,750**

Grand Total: $74,750

Note: a project such as this one usually lasts 12 to 18 months.

Set a working budget (possibly a per-piece budget) and let the gallery know at the outset what the guidelines are. This saves both you and the gallery time and energy. You'll be able to focus on items that are comfortably within the range of your budget. Buy the best quality possible in whatever category you like. You will appreciate the quality for years. Don't hesitate to do some comparison shopping. Although each art object is unique in itself, you may find another piece in the same style that you enjoy equally as well.

The best dealers understand budgets, and respect your desire to get good quality at a fair price. They are happy to work with enthusiastic clients who want to incorporate beautiful art into their lives.

Only deal with dealers who are helpful and present their art fairly. If you feel intimidated in a gallery, or feel the dealer isn't giving you the time and information you deserve to make intelligent choices, visit another gallery. Never buy art under pressure from a dealer, or to meet a deadline imposed by your interior design timetable.

GO TO AN AUCTION HOUSE

Attending an auction is an excellent way to learn about decorative arts, develop and add to a collection, and simply have a good time. Whether you attend as a buyer, seller, or observer, an auction is an experience that will enrich your understanding and enjoyment of the art and antiques world.

If you're a novice, it's important to choose a well-established auction house with a reputation for reliability. Try to be a patient observer and learn about the process as well as the value of items you may be interested in later on.

Buy a copy of the catalog and attend the viewing prior to the beginning of the auction itself. Each item, or "lot," that will be available for sale at the auction will be listed, and a professional estimate of selling price will be included. Professionals will be available during the viewing to answer questions and help you become familiar with the art objects as well as the process.

CHOOSING AN AUCTION

Find out about interesting auctions from the proprietors of galleries you like, or ask to be added to the mailing list of a reputable auction house. With these sources of information, you'll be informed of events that will feature quality items of interest to you. The established auction houses that have earned a reputation for reliability and expertise generally have a single location where they hold their auctions. Sometimes an auction will be held at an estate site, or a seller's location.

Before attending the auction, spend some time researching the art or antique you're interested in bidding on, so you'll be informed about its value and can make an informed decision. Talk to people at the galleries. Visit Internet sites to research your interests, or for information on upcoming auctions and recent auction prices. There also are books available that publish recent auction sales to help you get an idea of price and availability. Check your library or bookseller for publications like Gordon's Price Annual.

There seems to be an air of mystery and sophistication that surrounds auctions, but don't let that discourage you from discovering the auction experience. They are enjoyable and educational for anyone who is interested in obtaining or learning about art and antiques.

BE REALISTIC

For many of us, an auction might seem an opportunity to pick up an item at a bargain price. Realize that there may be bargains to be found, but in general, auctioned items are sold for a fair price. There may be a "reserve price," which is a private agreement between the seller and the auctioneer on the amount of a minimum bid.

If you educate yourself about the category you're interested in, you'll be at an advantage at an auction. It's equally important to research the market value of any lot you may be considering. Remember that there is an auctioneer's commission of 10 to 15 percent of the hammer price, to be paid in addition to the purchase price, as well as applicable sales taxes.

While you won't end up making the top bid simply by tugging your ear, it's important to pay attention when you're bidding. Be aware of the way the auctioneer communicates with the bidders and always listen for the auctioneer's "fair warning" announcement just before the gavel falls. ■

Antiques

CARL MOORE ANTIQUES, INC ....**(713) 524-2502**
1610 Bissonnet, Houston   Fax:(713) 524-2535
See ad on page 238B, 238C
Website: www.carlmooreantiques.net
e-mail: info@carlmooreantiques.net

Art
Galleries

ALLART ....**(713) 526-3631**
2635 Revere, Houston   Fax:(713) 526-3631
See ad on page 238D
e-mail: allart@wt.net

ARDEN'S ....**(713) 522-5281**
1631 W. Alabama, Houston   Fax:(713) 529-4203
See ad on page 245
Website: www.ardensgallery.com
e-mail: ardens@sbcglobal.net

Houston's Premier
Home & Design
Sourcebook

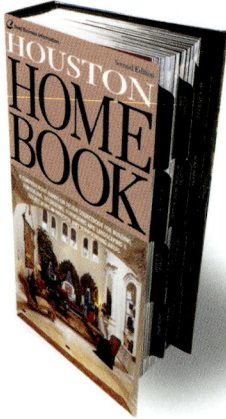

The ***Houston Home Book*** is your final destination when searching for home remodeling, building and decorating resources. This comprehensive, hands-on sourcebook to building, remodeling, decorating, furnishing and landscaping a luxury home is required reading for the serious and discriminating homeowner. With more than 300 full-color, beautiful pages, the ***Houston Home Book*** is the most complete and well-organized reference to the home industry. This hardcover volume covers all aspects of the process, includes listings of hundreds of industry professionals, and is accompanied by informative and valuable editorial discussing the most recent trends. Ordering your copy of the ***Houston Home Book*** now can ensure that you have the blueprints to your dream home, in your hand, today.

Visit our online store at
www.theashleygroup.com

O R D E R   F O R M

THE HOUSTON HOME BOOK

☐ YES, please send me _____ copies of the HOUSTON HOME BOOK at $39.95 per book, plus $4 Shipping & Handling per book.

Total amount enclosed: $_____   Please charge my: ☐ VISA   ☐ MasterCard   ☐ American Express

Card # _____   Exp. Date _____

Signature _____

Name _____   Phone (   ) _____

Address _____   E-mail _____

City _____   State _____   Zip Code _____

Send order to: Attn: Book Sales — Marketing, The Ashley Group — Reed Business Information 2000 Clearwater Drive, Oak Brook, IL 60523
Or Call Toll Free: 888.458.1750 Fax: 630.288.7949 E-mail ashleybooksales@reedbusiness.com

All orders must be accompanied by check, money order or credit card # for full amount. All book orders are nonrefundable.

ARCHITECTS

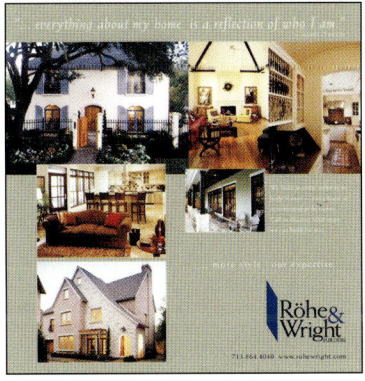

BUILDERS & REMODELERS

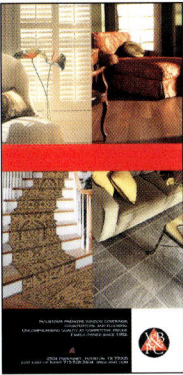

FLOORING

BEAUTIFULLY DESIGNED EDITORIAL PAGES

HOME FURNISHINGS

INTERIOR DESIGNERS

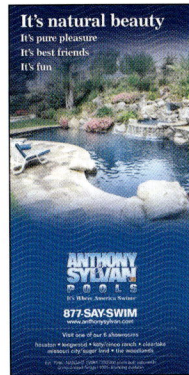

LANDSCAPERS

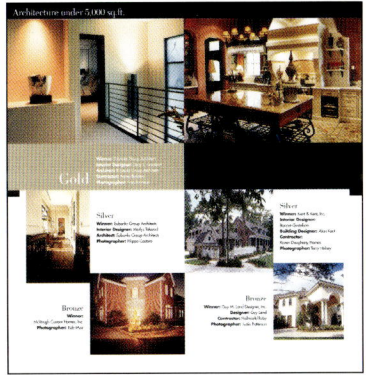

2002 HOME BOOK DESIGN EXCELLENCE AWARDS

Just a Sampling of the Spectacular pages in your Home Book

ART & ANTIQUES

Antique
In 1930 the U.S. Government ruled that objects had to be at least 100 years old to be classified as antiques, so they could be admitted duty free into the United States. Though it was a legislative tax decision, antiques have since been defined as objects made before 1830. Except for Indian artifacts, a few Spanish buildings in the Southwest, and a few French buildings in the Southeast, the oldest American antiques are but 300 years old.

Art Deco
Design style prevalent during the 1920s and 1930s, characterized by a sleek use of straight lines and slender form.

Art Nouveau
A decorative art movement that emerged in the late 19th century. Characterized by dense asymmetrical ornamentation in sinuous forms, it is often symbolic and of a sensous nature. Klimt worked in an Art Nouveau style.

Baroque
A movement in European painting in the 17th and early 18th centuries, characterized by violent movement, strong emotion, and dramatic lighting and coloring. Bernini, Caravaggio and Rubens were among important baroque artists.

Byzantine
A style of the Byzantine Empire and its provinces, c. 330-1450. Appearing mostly in religious mosaics, manuscript illuminations, and panel paintings, it is characterized by rigid, monumental, stylized forms with gold backgrounds.

Classicism
Referring to the principles of Greek and Roman art of antiquity with the emphasis on harmony, proportion, balance, and simplicity. In a general sense, it refers to art based on accepted standards of beauty.

Folk art
Works of a culturally homogeneous people without formal training, generally according to regional traditions and involving crafts.

Gothic
A European movement beginning in France. Gothic sculpture emerged c. 1200, Gothic painting later in the 13th century. The artworks are characterized by a linear, graceful, elegant style more naturalistic than that which had existed previously in Europe.

Minimalism
A movement in American painting and sculpture that originated in the late 1950s. It emphasized pure, reduced forms and strict, systematic compositions.

Rococo
An 18th century European style, originating in France. In reaction to the grandeur and massiveness of the baroque, rococo employed refined, elegant, highly decorative forms. Fragonard worked in this style.

Romanesque
A European style developed in France in the late 11th century. Its sculpture is ornamental, stylized and complex. Some Romanesque frescoes survive, painted in a monumental, active manner.

Romanticism
A European movement of the 18th to mid 19th century. In reaction to neoclassicism, it focused on emotion over reason, and on spontaneous expression. The subject matter was invested with drama and usually painted energetically in brilliant colors. Delacroix, Gericault, Turner, and Blake were Romantic artists.

BOOKS

Michigan-based architect Dominick Tringali uses the skill and knowledge that has brought him over 20 industry awards to share strategies on building the ultimate dream house. By combining unique concepts with innovative techniques and materials, Dominick's portfolio displays an array of homes noted for their timeless appeal. This $45 million collection of elite, custom homes contains the residences of notable CEOs, lawyers, doctors and sports celebrities including Chuck O'Brien, Joe Dumars, Tom Wilson, Larry Wisne and Michael Andretti.

RESIDENTIAL ARCHITECTURE:
LIVING PLACES
144 pages
9" x 12"
Art & Architecture
1-58862-088-3
$39.95   Hardcover

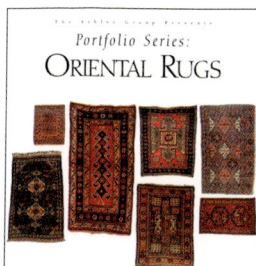

Top rug dealers throughout the country are profiled to provide helpful hints to successfully choose a rug that best suits a buyer's needs. Readers will also gain an understanding of the key elements to consider when purchasing an Oriental rug. Over 100 images will help a potential buyer get a feel for the styles and patterns available through each dealer. Additionally, this book provides a solid directory of vendors who hold invaluable expertise in this arena.

PORTFOLIO SERIES:
ORIENTAL RUGS
July 2003
150 pages
10" x 10"
Home Design
1-58862-987-2
$29.95   Hardcover

itles on luxury home style, design and architecture

888.458.1750

Home Books

12 Tips
For Pursuing Quality

1. Assemble a Team of Professionals During Preliminaries.
Search out and value creativity.

2. Educate Yourself on What to Expect.
But also be prepared to be flexible in the likely event of setbacks.

3. Realize the Value and Worth of Design.
It's the best value for your investment.

4. Be Involved in the Process.
It's more personally satisfying and yields the best results.

5. Bigger Isn't Better – Better is Better.
Look for what produces quality and you'll never look back.

6. Understand the Process.
Be aware of products, prices and schedules, to be a productive part of the creative team.

7. Present a Realistic Budget.
Creative, workable ideas can be explored.

8. Create the Right Environment.
Mutual respect, trust and communication get the job done.

9. There Are No Immediate Miracles.
Time is a necessary component in the quest for quality.

10. Have Faith in Yourself.
Discover your own taste and style.

11. Plan for the Future.
Lifestyles and products aren't static.

12. Do Sweat the Details.
Establish the discipline to stay organized.

HOUSTON HOME BOOK

10900 Northwest Freeway, Suite 122, Houston, TX 77092   713.263.0471 FAX 713.263.1927

Alphabetical Index

Professional Index

Architecture

Professional Index

260

261

Professional Index

262

Professional Index

263

Professional Index

Kitchen & Bath

Professional Index

267

Notes

268

269

271

HOME
THEATER
&
TECHNOLOGY

VIDEO

TOSHIBA

JVC

PANASONIC

LUCE

FUJITSU

NEC

AUDIO

SUNFIRE

ADCOM

DENON

**HARMON/
KARDON**

ONKYO

- Multi-Room Audio
- Prewire & Home Automation
- Custom Home Theater
- In-Wall Speakers
- Plasma & HDTV's
- Home Theater Seating

SPEAKERS

VELODYNE

MIRAGE

TANNOY

PINNACLE

R.B.H.

JBL

Showroom By
Appointment
Only

BRING THE MOVIES HOME TO YOU.

Houston Home Theatre Is Giving You A Reason To Add Excitement To Your Home

- Top name electronics such as JBL, Harmon Kardon, Panasonic
- Interior Design by the world's premier home theater designer
- Formerly known as the Owens Corning Visionaire FX Personal Entertainment

Enjoy theatre quality visuals and sound in the comfort of your own home. Now you can have the best in home entertainment at an affordable price. When we are through, you will be applauding even before watching a movie! For more information contact Houston Home Theatre, Inc. for a tour of this Personal Entertainment Center.

Contact Us Today For A Personal Consultation
713-686-4446
Houston Home Theatre
6815 NORTHAMPTON WAY • HOUSTON, TEXAS 77055

The Touch of a Button

If you had been able to show someone from only a generation ago a home of today, where every function and feature is integrated and instantly accessible, he surely would have thought it to be the stuff of science fiction. Today's luxury homes can respond to the needs of those within as if instinctively the homes know what is needed at every moment. Whether it be a hallway that lights as people enter or tile floors that warm just when a homeowner steps out of bed in the morning, today's luxury homes can be programmed to respond to every action of the inhabitants.

At a time when families are directing their activities into the home, home theater and sound systems provide them with all the more reason to stay in.

Home theaters, where family and friends can gather to watch their favorite films and big-ticket sporting events in comfort, rival commercial theaters in their visual and aural experience. Homes today have to be wired to accommodate the rapid changes in audio-video technology. Whereas just a few years ago technicians were installing awe-inspiring CD systems that could hold hundreds of discs, homeowners today are converting their music collections to mp3 files, that can be accessed from any place in the home, through an easy to navigate keypad. These technological advances turn our homes from mere shelters into expressions of our lifestyles.

Photo courtesy of **Bang & Olufsen America, Inc.**

Home Theater & Technology

THE IMPORTANCE OF A HOME THEATER DESIGN SPECIALIST

Home theater is widely specified as a custom home feature today. The sophisticated homeowner with a well-developed eye (and ear) for quality demands the latest technology in a home entertainment system that will provide pleasure for many years. Because of the fluid marketplace, the vast possibilities of the future, and the complexity of the products, it's crucial to employ an established professional to design and install your home theater.

The experts presented on the following pages can advise you on the best system for your home. They can find an appropriate entertainment center, masterly install your system, and teach you to use it. Their expertise will make the difference.

THE HOME THEATER DESIGN PROCESS

Tell your builder or remodeling specialist early on if you want a home theater, especially if built-in speakers or a ceiling-mounted video projection unit are part of the plan.

Inform the interior designer so proper design elements can be incorporated. Window treatments to block out light and help boost sound quality, furnishings or fabrics to hide or drape speakers, and comfortable seating to enhance the media experience should be considered. If you plan to control the window treatments by remote control, these decisions will have to be coordinated.

When visiting showrooms, be ready to answer these questions:

• What is your budget? There is no upper limit.

• Do you want a High Definition Television (HDTV) or projection video system? A DVD player? Built-in or free-standing speakers?

• Do you want Internet access for your television?

• What style of cabinetry and lighting do you want? Do you want specialized lighting? A built-in bar? How much storage is needed?

• What are the seating requirements? Seating should be at least seven feet from the screen.

• Do you want whole-house control capability so you can distribute and control the system from different rooms of the house?

• How will you incorporate the system with the rest of the room? Must the room meet other needs?

• Do you want extra luxuries, like multiple screens, or a remote control system that allows you to dim the lights and close the draperies?

PLAN AHEAD

Even if you aren't installing a home theater system right away, have a room designed to serve that purpose later. Get the wiring done and build the room an appropriate shape and size. Get the right antenna. Ask for double drywall for noise control.

SAVE AN AISLE SEAT

For the best seat in the house, your home theater will need the following:
A large screen television and/or projection video system (from 32-inch direct view up to 200-inches, depending on the size of the room). New, compact products are available now.
A surround-sound receiver to direct sound to the appropriate speaker with proper channel separation.
A surround-sound speaker system, with front, rear, and center channel speakers and a sub-woofer for powerful bass response.
A comfortable environment, ideally a rectangular room with extra drywall to block out distractions.

• Will this room function in the future? As technology continues to change our lifestyle, plan for this room to grow and change as well. Ask your salesperson for advice.

Home theaters are installed at the same time as security and phone systems, before insulation and drywall. In new construction or remodeling, start making decisions at least two months before the drywall is hung. Allow four weeks for delivery and installation.

AUTOMATED HOME MANAGEMENT

It's like clockwork: Your alarm clock wakes you, and while you are rubbing the sleep from your eyes, a path from your bed to the master bath to the kitchen is lit for you. The stone floor of your bath has warmed and the climates of the rooms you'll be walking through this morning are all in sync. Once your eyes have opened, you walk to the kitchen, where a hot, fresh, pot of coffee is waiting for you and the television is already tuned to your favorite morning news program. Once you've left home, there's no need to worry about whether you've locked all of the doors or have turned the lights off, because those things are also handled automatically. But just in case, for your own peace of mind, you can check on the status of your home's locks, lights and windows from a remote computer or even a cell phone, and lock, close or turn off whatever you may have forgotten about.

Such are the advantages of automated home management. Home automation brings an added, virtually impenetrable layer of ease and security to the home. Energy can be saved by keeping the heat or air-conditioning at a low level while you're out of the house, then as you're on the way home from the office or your daily errands, you can bring the home climate back to your comfort level. Criminals can be thwarted by lighting that not only automatically switches on at night, but comes on at random times, in random rooms, to make it look as if your home is "lived in" when you're away.

You don't have to be a computer wizard to operate these automated home systems. Voice recognition software allows you to simply say, "Turn lights on at 7 p.m. for four hours," and it's done. Systems have become smarter: while a direct line to the police department can be activated by an object coming into contact with a door or window at 3 a.m., the homeowner, while at the office or the golf course, can be alerted first when something is detected at 3 p.m. A quick check on any computer, which will give him or her a view from the home's security cameras, can let the homeowner know that the afternoon incident was caused by children who have been told not to play soccer so close to the house.

While it all may have seemed unbelievably futuristic not long ago, modern home technology is making homeowner's lives easier, more peaceful and much more enjoyable. ∎

YOUR PERSONAL SCREENING ROOM

Here's an example of the costs involved with outfitting a room in the mid- to high-scale price range for a home theater
Labor (at $55/hour): $3,500
50-inch television: $4,000
DVD player: $900
Amplifier with surround-sound decoder: $10,000
Six speakers with subwoofer: $10,000
Satellite dish (high definition): $1,000
Delivery/installation: $2,500
Seating: Eight leather module seats, $15,000
Infrared sensors to control lighting, motorized drapes, security system: $10,000

Total: $57,000

BEST TIP:

Have phone lines, DSL or cable modems connected to every TV outlet in the house for Internet access and satellite reception.

Home Theater
Design

HOME THEATER STORE ....**(713) 952-5700**
   5805 Westheimer, Houston   Fax:(713) 952-8877
   See ad on page C2, 253
   <u>Website:</u> www.hometheaterstore.com
   <u>e-mail:</u> prashant@hometheaterstore.com

HOUSTON HOME THEATER ....**(713) 686-4446**
   6815 Northampton Way, Ste. 100, Houston   Fax:(713) 682-1554
   See ad on page 248D

SHERRY RENFROW MOORE'S DESIGNER SHOWCASE ....**(281) 494-7469**
   12705 S. Kirkwood, Ste. 211, Stafford   Fax:(281) 242-2628
   See ad on page 136D, 255, C3
   <u>Website:</u> www.designershowcasewow.com
   <u>e-mail:</u> general@designershowcasewow.com

VISION AUDIO...**(281) 681-1373**
   26009 Budde Rd., Suite B-400, The Woodlands   Fax:(281) 292-5291
   See ad on page 248B, 248C
   <u>Website:</u> www.visionaudiotx.com
   <u>e-mail:</u> sean@visionaudiotx.com

The Ashley Group Luxury Home Resource Collection

The Ashley Group (www.theashleygroup.com) is pleased to offer as your final destination when searching for home improvement and luxury resources the following **Home Books** in your local market. Available now: *Seattle, Boston, San Francisco Bay Area, Orange County, Kansas City, Connecticut/Westchester County and Houston among others.* These comprehensive, hands-on guides to building, remodeling, decorating, furnishing, and landscaping a luxury home, are required reading for the serious and selective homeowner. With more than 400 full-color, beautiful pages, the **Home Book** series in each market covers all aspects of the building and remodeling process, including listings of hundreds of local industry professionals, accompanied by informative and valuable editorial discussing the most recent trends.

Order your copies today and make your dream come true!

Sherry Renfrow Moore's
Designer Showcase
P: 281.494.7469

TX Licensed #5573

HOME THEATER

Ambience synthesis
Using surround sound technology and various matrixed or digital music or film modes to create the feel or ambience associated with a space other than the one in which the sounds are being heard.

Amplifier
Electronic component that accepts a low-level signal and recreates the signal with more power; this term is most often used in audio/video to describe an audio component which takes in line-level audio signals through interconnect cables and outputs a high-powered replica of the input in order to drive speakers and create sound.

DVD
Compact disc sized, 5-inch diameter optical disc capable of holding digital video and audio information for movies, music, computer games and more.

Laserdisc
Large 12-inch diameter optical digital format used for playing back images and sound. The laserdisc was the precursor to the DVD, offering superior video and sound capabilities compared to any available consumer video format prior to DVD.

Plasma television
A flat, shallow, light-weight television system that uses gas excited by an electric pulse to give off ultraviolet rays which in turn excite red, green and blue phosphors to generate an image.

Preamplifier
Audio component that adjusts the volume of an audio signal and performs switching functions between attached input devices and an amplifier or group of amplifiers. The preamplifier's primary task is volume control and source control.

Surround channel speaker
Speaker used to reproduce surround channel information primarily to create ambience and sonic realism. Surround channel speakers are usually hung on a wall or ceiling to the sides of the listener or behind the listener.

Matrix surround sound
Method of encoding more than two channels of audio into a pair of analog audio channels. Matrix surround sound is encoded during production and decoded by the proper surround sound processor. The most widely used form of matrix surround sound is Dolby Pro-Logic with Dolby Surround used to a lesser degree.

THX
Set of specifications and certifications designed by Lucasfilm Ltd. to ensure optimum reproduction of movie sound and video in movie theaters and home theaters (Home THX program).

Tuner
Electronic device used to receive transmissions in the form of electromagnetic waves and decode from those signals useable audio or video information that can be reproduced by an audio or video system.

INDEXES

DESIGN

The following design books represent the premier works of selected designers, luxury homebuilders and architects.

This book is divided into 10 chapters, starting with design guidelines in regard to color, personality and collections. In these chapters, interior designer Perla Lichi presents beautiful, four-color photographs of the design commissions she has undertaken for clients accompanied by informative editorial on the investment value of professional interior design.

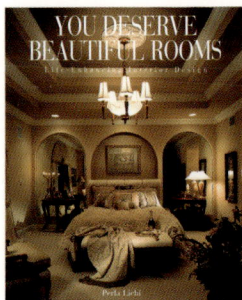

YOU DESERVE BEAUTIFUL ROOMS
120 pages, 9.75" x 14"
Home Design, Architecture
1-58862-016-6 $39.95   Hardcover

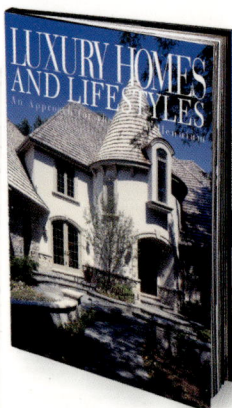

Orren Pickell is renowned as one of the nation's finest builders of custom homes. In this collection of more than 80 beautiful four-color photos and drawings, Pickell shows off some of his finest creations to give homeowners unique ideas on building a new home or adding to an existing one.

LUXURY HOMES & LIFESTYLES
120 pages, 9.75" x 14"
Architecture, Home Design
0-9642057-4-2 $39.95   Hardcover

Designer Susan Fredman has spent 25 years creating interiors, which, in one way or another, have been inspired by nature. In this book, she takes readers through rooms which reflect elements of our surroundings as they are displayed throughout the year.

AT HOME WITH NATURE
136 pages, 11.25" x 11.25"
Home Design, Architecture
1-58862-043-3 $39.95   Hardcover

The Ashley Group is proud to present these speci

CALL TO ORDER